PRAYER IN THE NEW TESTAMENT

Make Your Requests Known to God

Helen and Leonard Doohan

A Michael Glazier Book
THE LITURGICAL PRESS
Collegeville, Minnesota

A Michael Glazier Book published by The Liturgical Press

Cover design by David Manahan, O.S.B.

1	2	3	4	5	6	7	8	9	10

Library of Congress Cataloging-in-Publication Data

Doohan, Helen.
    Prayer in the New Testament : make your requests known to God /
Helen Doohan, Leonard Doohan.
        p.   cm.
    ''A Michael Glazier book.''
    Includes bibliographical references.
    ISBN 0-8146-5007-4
    1. Bible. N.T.—Prayers. 2. Prayer—Biblical teaching.
3. Intercessory prayer—Biblical teaching. I. Doohan, Leonard.
II. Title.
BS2545.P67.D66   1991
248.3'2—dc20
                                                91-35750
                                                   CIP

We dedicate this book to Ken Liona

CONTENTS

ACKNOWLEDGMENTS

Scripture texts used in this work are taken from *The New Testament, New International Version.* International Bible Society, 1973, 1978, 1984.

"Scripture and Contemporary Spirituality" (I Chap. 3) is based on an article in *Spirituality Today* 42 (1990): 62-74, and is used here with permission of the editor.

stand these prayers of request when we see them within the larger perspective and context of the Gospels and other expressions of New Testament prayer. In other words, the situations, experiences, and developments in the time of Jesus, disciples, and early Church actually condition the direction of intercessory prayer.

Prayer of request goes beyond the pious requests associated with early stages of Christian growth to intercession that challenges us to deeper faith, enduring hope, and mutual love. As we courageously respond to the biblical models of prayerful persons and communities, we "offer our requests to God" with the deeper insight that we challenge ourselves in the very experience of our prayer. Our prayer becomes transformational; our requests translate into Christian life and ministry that actualize our prayer.

Prayer in the New Testament attempts to guide the reader through the various stages and dimensions of biblical prayer, with a secondary focus on the prayer of request. We divide the book into four major sections: (1) Scripture and Prayer, (2) Models of Intercessory Prayer, (3) The Gospels' Focus on the Prayer of Request, and (4) The Church Community's Life of Prayer. Short chapters develop each of the topics, expanding the basic theme. In the section on "Scripture and Prayer" we examine the relationship between prayer and spirituality as a basis for living out the biblical message in our times. The experience of God within the New Testament writings and the emphasis on prayer in the Church's contemporary reflection on its mission, Vatican II, remind us of the centrality of prayer to our Christian existence. For "Models of Prayer" we look to Jesus, Paul, and the apostolic prayer of the early Church. Each example potentially expands our notion of prayer, its qualities, its varied expressions, and its ability to foster growth in ourselves and our communities. In "The Gospels' Focus on the Prayer of Request" we examine each Gospel in its setting. In Mark's community, living through a period of uncertainty, prayer becomes punctuated by urgency and struggle. Matthew addresses the divisions within the community, orienting his teaching on prayer to needs for reconciliation. In Luke, Jesus becomes the model of prayer, teaching through word and example, while John challenges his Church to pray in loving union with the Lord. The final section of the book, ''The Church Community's Life of Prayer,'' examines the Church's life of prayer in times of trial, turning attention to its identity as a prayerful Church. The Eucharist, communion with Jesus and the Father, and attentiveness to the Spirit who prays within us bring the biblical development of prayer full circle.

The progression of the book moves us from general introductory reflections, to models that tell us where we are and where we are going, to the Gospels that insert us into the life situations of each community and the author's response to community needs by interpretation of the message of Jesus. The ecclesial community prays in changing times, using different expressions and praying in union with Father, Son, and Spirit.

Prayer of request, an underlying theme, becomes a life of union with and sensitivity to the Spirit within us. Our request becomes more expansive and inclusive as we mature in faith because it is an expression of who we are and who we are becoming as women and men of the Church.

Readers can follow the progression of the book or select chapters to suit their needs. Readings follow the four main sections. Our hope is that each chapter will offer a wider perspective on prayer for the reader and a challenge for growth both personally and as members of the ecclesial community.

PART I:
SCRIPTURE AND PRAYER

CHAPTER ONE
Experiences of God in Scripture

In the letter to the Romans, a writing that precedes the Gospels, Paul proclaims: "Oh, the depth of the riches of the wisdom and knowledge of God! How unsearchable his judgments, and his paths beyond tracing out! Who has known the mind of the Lord? Or who has been his counselor? Who has ever given to God, that God should repay him [or her]? For from [God] and through [God] and to [God] are all things. To [God] be the glory forever! Amen" (Rom 11:33-36). Centuries later, a Spanish mystic, John of the Cross, wrote, "Never seek to satisfy yourself in what you know of God, but rather in what you don't know about him; never stop to love or to take delight in what you know or experience of God, but love and take delight in what you cannot understand and experience of him." The insights of these two great figures touch the mystery of God by emphasizing the unknown, the depth, the incomprehensibleness of the Lord God. Paul of Tarsus and John of the Cross also understand that we can be profoundly transformed by mystery as we experience some dimension of it in our own lives. In fact, the words of writers on the experience of God are far more significant in what they do not say about the mystery of God or Christ than in what they do say. We realize that the meaning of the mysteries of faith far surpasses any words we use to express them.

Why do we as Christians presume that an experience of God is open to us? Where and how do we experience God? What attitudes prepare us for this encounter with the Lord? What are the biblical models that provide substance for our reflection? What results do we expect from this encounter with the divine? These questions naturally arise because of the close connection between the experience of God and prayer. We must address this possibility of experiencing God if we are to identify the focus of our prayer and to gain insight into the prayer of request. However, such questions about the essence of existence, while easily asked, elicit few comprehensive responses.

1. The Experience of the Divine

As Christians, we assume that an experience of God is possible. This assumption requires faith, a gift from the God who actively pursues us. Without the insight of faith, access to God in the world, in the word of Scripture, and through others, is impossible. Our belief sensitizes us to the multiple indications of God's presence so that we see reality alive with God and become filled with wonder and awe.

Scripture provides a specific access to God, telling us stories, in religious language and symbol, about believers' experience of God and its significance in the life of the Jewish and Christian community. This experience of God, in the New Testament, offers insight into God's special revelation in Jesus, which gives direction and meaning to life. Biblical spirituality suggests that we come in contact with the essence of life as we journey in faith through the Scripture. This in-depth listening is a quality of prayer that enables us to glimpse the ultimate meaning behind all things. However, Christians encounter God with their own personalities, giving this potentially universal experience of the divine personal and unique characteristics. Life itself opens us to the presence of God, and as our receptivity to this gift of the Lord grows, so does our experience. God is close to us; our awareness of the divine presence needs to grow.

2. Attitudes in Approaching the Experience of God

When using Scripture as a basis to identify aspects of the experience of God, we not only examine the text and the particular circumstances surrounding the composition of the text that affect its meaning, but we listen to, read, and interpret the message as twentieth century participants in this biblical revelation. The God of history speaks to our personal, ecclesial, and contemporary history. Once we understand the essence of God's revelation in the biblical text through examination of the language, history, theology, and strategy of the author, then we can interpret its meaning for today. In faith, we thus respond to the revelation of the Lord.

Apart from understanding how to approach the biblical text, other attitudes open us to an authentic experience of God. Perhaps the primary quality is that of directing attention towards God. This attention can be intense, creating a desire within the person that almost draws God into our experience, or more correctly, opens us to God's abiding presence in our midst. Attention to the transcendent leads to awareness, but also to a new openness so that we are ready to hear God's new revelation. Although the dialogue of prayer is important, talking *to* God can be an obstacle to the experience *of* God and the divine intervention in our lives. Attention and openness are far more important dimensions for an experience of God than dialogue.

Presence, particularly to the current moment, is a quality conducive to the experience of the transcendent. Particular circumstances activate this ability to be present, namely situations of trust, love, peace, and joy. Likewise, the ability to concentrate, direct attention, and focus puts us in potential contact with an experience of God. These quality moments foster within us the ability to discover the Lord's presence in every moment of life. In faith, we begin to identify God's presence even when God seems absent or distant. Experiencing each

moment of life becomes an experience of the real presence of
the Lord who calls us to new life.

Another facet of the experience of God is our ability to enter
into deep, satisfying relationships with others. In these circumstances, we grow in and because of mutual relationships. We
slowly develop the freedom to be truly influenced by another
and to receive love. The way we approach these human relationships is an indication of how we enter into a relationship
with God. Attitudes in prayer are essentially life attitudes,
demonstrating the connection between prayer and life. Qualities that foster mutual love, freedom, and interdependence
become the attributes that can lead us to a mature experience
of prayer.

As Christian believers, we know that God reveals the divine self to us in the world, through the word and through
others. The approaches we cultivate in order to understand
the essence of life are the very approaches that will be conducive to a quality experience of God who continually acts in
our lives. The ability to direct attention, be present, and enter
into mutual relationships with others, develops the attitudes
that will lead to a profound experience of the Lord.

3. Biblical Experiences of God

Underlying the biblical narrative is the community's awareness of God acting on its behalf. Christians experience God
as the one who calls, who is present, who transforms, and who
reveals. This unfolding story comes to us through the various
figures we meet in the New Testament: primarily Jesus, but
also the disciples who follow in faith. Special events also reveal aspects of God to us, namely baptism, conversion, ritual
prayer, transfiguration. All these potential theophanies or
manifestations identify aspects of God and our response to this
revelatory experience in prayer.

Experiencing the God who calls. In the opening pages of the
Synoptic Gospels, Matthew and Luke, like Mark, reflect on
the call of Jesus: "At that time Jesus came from Nazareth in
Galilee and was baptized by John in the Jordan. As Jesus was

coming up out of the water, he saw heaven being torn open and the Spirit descending on him like a dove. And a voice came from heaven: 'You are my Son, whom I love; with you I am well pleased' " (Mark 1:9-11; *see* Matt 3:13-17; Luke 3:21-22). The wilderness setting of the baptism and temptation scenes reminds us of God's call of Israel and indicates the divine dimension in which Jesus acts. The call of Jesus leads to the proclamation of the good news of the kingdom, the beginning of public ministry, and his invitation to others to share in his life: " 'The time has come,' he said. 'The kingdom of God is near. Repent and believe the good news!' "(Mark 1:15).

Jesus' first disciples hear the Lord's call while involved in their usual life situations. They not only recognize a special call, but respond immediately and totally with their work and family relationships, transformed by this invitation to follow Jesus (Mark 1:16-20). Simon, Andrew, James, John, later the Twelve, and other women and men who follow Jesus become involved in ministry, a ministry of gathering the community and serving the needs of others through word and work. Just as Jesus' call leads to the proclamation that God's kingdom is at hand, so too the call of the disciples leads to their lived proclamation of the presence of God.

The God who calls invites us to a new level of life, since the awareness of call leads to personal transformation and service of the community. Response to the experience of God's call is a life response and the formulation of our prayers of request often reflects this call and response.

Experiencing the God Who is Present. As Jesus and the disciples travel throughout Galilee, they minister specifically through their proclamation, teaching, and healing: "They went to Capernaum, and when the Sabbath came, Jesus went into the synagogue and began to teach. The people were amazed at his teaching, because he taught them as one who had authority, not as the teachers of the law" (Mark 1:21-22). People responded to what they heard and saw: "The people were all so amazed that they asked each other, 'What is this? A new teaching—and with authority! He even gives orders to evil spirits and they obey him' " (Mark 1:27). Individuals requested his healing touch: "A man with leprosy came to him and begged him on his knees, 'If you are willing, you can make me clean' " (Mark 1:40). This preaching and healing of Jesus indicate another dimension of the presence of God.

In response to faith, Jesus not only heals but forgives sins, leading to the question posed by the scribes: "Who can forgive sins but God alone?" (Mark 2:7). Those who observed the power at work in Jesus, "were amazed and glorified God," saying, "We never saw anything like this" (Mark 2:12). While some people feared God's power at work in Jesus (Mark 3:6; 5:17), the disciples had a different response: "And they were filled with awe, and said to one another, 'Who is this, that the wind and sea obey him?' " (Mark 4:41). Mark's Gospel attempts to respond to this inquiry in Peter's confession: "You are the Christ" (Mark 8:29). In like manner, a centurion also professes his faith in saying, "Truly this man was the Son of God" (Mark 15:39).

The earliest Gospel testifies to the presence of God in Jesus. Later, Matthew and Luke will develop the realization that God's promises are fulfilled in Jesus, and John will indicate that Jesus and the Father are one. The New Testament writers reflect again and again on the presence of the risen Lord and the continual presence of Jesus through the power of the Spirit. The indications of the presence of God in Jesus' words and works become the proclamation of belief by the early Christians who experience God in Jesus. However, the description of this transcendent experience, in all the biblical narratives, is not ethereal or only conceptual but concrete and real in the person Jesus. The word becomes flesh and through flesh we experience the Word of God.

Experiencing the God Who Transforms. Conversion is a transformational experience and, in the case of someone like Paul, an event so central for him and for the Church that Paul not only refers to it in his letters (Gal 1:11-17; 1 Cor 9:1; 15:8-10; Phil 3:4-11; Rom 1:5; 2 Cor 4:1-6; 5:16), but Luke also gives three accounts of the tradition (Acts 9:1-19; 22:4-16; 26:12-18). In all the accounts, God takes the initiative in the choice of Paul as Apostle to the Gentiles. As Paul reflects on this call, his religious consciousness changes and he becomes a prophet and a servant of the Lord as a believer in Jesus.

While different interpretations of the conversion exist, Paul himself never speaks of the inner event, but only its effect, his mission to the Gentiles. His conversion moves Paul, the zealous Pharisee, into service of the Church on an equal basis with Peter and other early Christian missionaries. He establishes churches, communities of faith, but he also discovers a deeper meaning in the conversion event. Paul's awareness of the mystery of the relationship between Christ and Christians results from the question, "Why are you persecuting me?" (Acts 9:4-5). This eventually leads Paul to speak about Christians being "in Christ" and Christ in them.

Paul's experience of God includes a transformational revelation: the realization of the union of Christ with believers and the presence of Christ in the community of believers. This insight leads to Paul's ceaseless missionary endeavors in the early Church; thus, his religious experience results in mission and ministry.

Experiencing the God Who Reveals. The experience of God by New Testament figures consistently affirms Jesus as beloved Son, the presence of God in Jesus, and the union of Christ and believers. Other episodes such as the transfiguration accounts (Mark 9:1-8; Matt 17:1-8; Luke 9:28-36) and the feeding episodes (Mark 6:30-44; 8:1-10; Matt 14:13-21; 15:32-39; Luke 9:12-17; John 6:1-15) contain unique insights for those who approach the biblical texts from the perspective of faith. Both of these events qualify as theophanies, manifestations of the transcendent Lord, reminiscent of Sinai/Horeb (Exod 24:16; 33:19-22; I Kgs 19:11). Both reveal the glory of God in Jesus.

"After six days Jesus took Peter, James, and John with him and led them up a high mountain, where they were all alone. There he was transfigured before them. His clothes became dazzling white, whiter than anyone in the world could bleach them. . . . Then a cloud appeared and enveloped them, and a voice came from the cloud: 'This is my Son, whom I love. Listen to him!' Suddenly, when they looked around, they no longer saw anyone with them except Jesus" (Mark 9:2-3, 7-8).

This revelation echoes Jesus' baptism account and anticipates the fuller revelation of the resurrection and parousia. While the transfiguration is potentially a time of true recognition of Jesus and a source of strengthening for what lies ahead, namely suffering and death, this vision is incomprehensible to the disciples in Mark. Their failure to understand and their fear would change to enlightenment and hope only with the coming of the Spirit (Acts 2:1-4; 14-28). While the transfiguration is a powerful revelation for us, there is a delayed impact on the earliest followers. The revelation inherent in profound religious experiences often needs reflection, testing, and guidance by the Spirit after the event itself.

The feeding episodes in Mark also lead to a similar response. The disciples fail to understand the revelation (Mark 6:52; 8:21) and do not understand the significance of the actions. The fullness of this revelation remains substantially veiled until the writing of John's Gospel. However, the disciples do experience Jesus as the shepherd (Mark 6:34), showing compassion for the crowd (Mark 8:2) by his generous feeding of them with his teaching as well as with bread. The feeding episodes culminate in the Last Supper account (Mark 14:12-25) that indicates the extent of the Lord's self-gift for humanity: " 'This is my blood of the covenant, which is poured out for many,' he said to them" (Mark 14:24). John reflects further on the meaning of the Eucharistic revelation by indicating its consequences for the followers of Jesus: "Now that I, your Lord and Teacher, have washed your feet, you also should wash one another's feet. I have set you an example that you should do as I have done for you" (John 13:14-15). The God who reveals shows divine involvement in an experience of religious significance and prophetic human action. The content of this revelation suggests a new understanding of Jesus who is truly bread and life for us, and a manifestation of the glory of God. It also clearly demonstrates that Eucharist, rightly understood, expresses itself in service.

The New Testament experience of God comes to us primarily through our understanding of Jesus. When we reflect on Jesus and his actions on our behalf, we recognize God's presence with us. The experience of God becomes crystallized in our reflection on concrete biblical narratives, suggesting God's continued presence in Jesus through the Spirit and in the believing community, the Church. Likewise, the biblical accounts of the experience of God develop a consciousness of mission that results in the service of others. The fruits of the experience, rather than the experience itself, command the attention of the New Testament writers. Perhaps this insight represents the heart of the Bible's teaching for us and suggests the substance of our prayers of request.

4. The Experience of God and Its Relationship to Prayer

Our experience of God affects our prayer, but our prayer opens us to a fuller experience of God who continually manifests life to us. The New Testament image of a God who calls, is present, transforms, and reveals is best understood when we focus on the person Jesus. We experience God in Jesus; we discover the meaning of prayer in the prayer of Jesus.

Both an experience of the divine and of prayer have some common attributes, requiring of us attention, presence, openness, faith, and trust. Both result primarily from the Lord's initiative and gift to us, rather than from our preparations for the event. Furthermore, both the experience of God and of prayer concern the present moment, but they also recall the past and prepare us for the future. We glimpse the reality behind all things and we begin to understand the reality of ourselves as we live in the continued presence of God. We know the Lord works in and through us, for these religious moments lead to a renewed commitment that we manifest in service. The authenticity of our religious experience and prayer life is tested in the arena of living as we stand in the presence of our sisters and brothers. In fact, Scripture suggests that we not only experience God in life, but that our prayer in all its forms reflects our life situations. We pray that the presence of God becomes increasingly evident to us, and that we have the eyes to see. The contemplative insight of prayer becomes the ministry that reflects the faith of the contemplative, arousing wonder and new awareness for all those who would see.

Faith is the gift and starting point for prayer and for new experiences of God. But in faith, as in prayer, the initiative is always the Lord's. For the Christian who receives this gift, the most appropriate response is a life of total service of God and of others. The Christian prays that his or her response becomes a more authentic expression of this faith.

As readers of the Word of God in Scripture, we are convinced that we can and do experience God's action on our behalf and God's love manifested in the sending of the Lord Jesus. This experience continually opens us to new possibilities in prayer, but like the experience of God in Scripture, these possibilities are intimately connected to the reality of our lives, relationships, and world. If we are aware of God's presence with us today, we will experience the divine presence more fully tomorrow; for we touch only a minute portion of the unfathomable riches of God and delight in what we are just beginning to know. We make our requests to God to deepen this life within us.

CHAPTER TWO
A Church Alive with Scripture

1. Scripture in Vatican II

This section looks at the Second Vatican Council's challenge to intensify the role of Scripture in the experience and teachings of the Church and in the life of contemporary Christians. It forms a basis for our reflection on prayer.

1. Scripture in Vatican II

Most of the documents of the Second Vatican Council are deductive documents. They draw their major conclusions from the basic principles and teachings of Scripture. The Council's documents offer innumerable references to Scripture, but, more important still, they immerse readers in scriptural themes, teaching, images, ideals, and promises. The general atmosphere is totally scriptural. Vatican Council II is not a complex of teachings distinct from Scripture, but rather the present day Church's reinterpretation and reincarnation of Scripture for us and our contemporary needs.

The Council was more than a prolonged study session or workshop. It was for the participants a total religious experience. The changes of attitude from session to session, observable in discussions and in the various editions of the documents, can be grouped into three major steps in a religious experience—a conversion process. These three steps correspond to major clarifications from Scripture. These three stages in the religious experience of the Council are as follows: first, the Church became aware of itself as a community; secondly, it became aware of itself as a community in the world; thirdly, it became aware of itself as a community in the world for the service of the world. These attitudinal changes were felt in every document. They arose from scriptural reflection on humankind as the people of God; on the incarnation of Jesus and the need for the ongoing incarnation of the Church; and on the Church as the servant people of a servant God. Here we see major reflection on Scripture leading to a conversion experience which modifies the whole direction of the Council. Moreover, nowadays, we cannot come to a lived knowledge of the Council unless we too move through this scripturally inspired conversion process.

Not only is the Council's teaching presented in an atmosphere steeped in Scripture, and its teaching the result of an experience inspired by scriptural reflection, but when we read documents' specific statements we find a profound synthesis of how the Church becomes alive through Scripture.

The document on Revelation affirms that sacred Scripture is like "a mirror in which the pilgrim Church on earth looks at God" (Revelation, 7:2). Elsewhere, "He is present in His word, since it is He Himself who speaks when the Holy Scriptures are read in the Church" (Liturgy, 7:1). Because of this conviction the Church as a whole affirms that it "is concerned to move ahead daily towards a deeper understanding of the sacred Scriptures" (Revelation, 23:1).

The Council challenges people from every ministry and role in the Church to a deeper and more prayerful reading of Scripture. Bishops and priests must diligently read and carefully study the Bible (Revelation, 25:1) so that, as it says elsewhere, all their knowledge will be "drawn primarily from reading and meditating on the sacred Scriptures" (Priests, 19:1). This reading, when accompanied by prayer (Revelation, 25:1), will be a strong support for the priestly life and ministry (Priests, 18:1).

The Council urges bishops in particular to see to it that all catechetical instruction be solidly based in Scripture (Bishops,

14:1), and it calls them to facilitate courses in Scripture for the continued updating of their priests (Bishops, 16:4).

In the training of seminarians the study of Scripture will be vital (Priestly Formation, 13), for Scripture must become the soul of all theology (Priestly Formation, 16:2). In fact, it is the guarantee of the continual rejuvenation of theological studies (Revelation, 24; Church, 67:2).

Not only does the Council emphasize the importance of Scripture for specific Church ministers, but one of the major documents insists that "Easy access to sacred Scripture should be provided for all the Christian faithful" (Revelation, 22:1). More concretely in the decree for laity, the Church states that all present day educational aids for laity should be "directed towards the acquisition of a deeper knowledge of sacred Scripture" (Laity, 32:1).

When the Council addresses the needs of the missions, we read that all the training of workers must be with an eye on Scripture (Missions, 16:3); when it gives advice to missionaries, we read that they should draw their strength principally from contact with the Scriptures (Missions, 26:1). When documents highlight religious' efforts for a deeper union with Christ, we read that "In the first place they should take the sacred Scriptures in hand each day by way of attaining 'the excelling knowledge of Jesus Christ' (Phil 3:8)" (Religious, 6:2).

Not only does the Council challenge all ministries and vocations to deepen their contact with Scripture, but all areas of the Church's life and involvement need the perspective and support of Scripture. While the Council challenges to renewal in priestly training, missions, and the study of theology, it also indicates that the roots of work for the union of the Churches are in scriptural awareness (Ecumenism, 17:1; 21). In fact, we discover not only ecumenical unity but also the general unity for which the Church works in a faithful reading of Scripture (Church, 15:1; Ecumenism, 3; 2; 5).

Turning to liturgy we find that Scripture reading and study are necessary for a good and clear understanding of Church worship (Liturgy, 16; 24). The content of the music must be drawn from Scripture (Liturgy, 121:3), and homilies based on Scripture (Liturgy, 35). We read that "The treasures of the Bible are to be opened up more lavishly, so that richer fare may be provided for the faithful at the table of God's Word'' (Liturgy, 51). Whether it be in liturgy or study we keep hearing phrases like ''Make Scripture more easily accessible'' (Liturgy, 92).

In addition to these specific statements, the Council gives entire chapters in its documents to ways of reading and studying Scripture (Revelation, III), and the place of Scripture in the life of the Church (Revelation, IV).

Perhaps we can best sum up the convictions of the Church—which makes the Council speak so much on this point—in the words of the document on Scripture: ''[Scripture is] the supreme rule of faith'' (Revelation, 21:1); and it is the perennial source of spiritual life.

The documents of Vatican II are based on Scripture; the experience of the Council was inspired by Scripture; the teaching of the Council forcefully challenges that every person and every area of involvement feel the effects of a studied and prayerful contact with the revealed word of God. Opening up the meaning of Scripture and the Council documents is a major challenge for the believing community. An understanding of spirituality can prepare us for the task and so we turn our attention to Christian spirituality.

Jesus will be spirit and life for us today only if we interpret and apply the Word.

Spirituality is a practical discipline that studies the vital activities that lead to the growth and maturity of Christian life. It is concerned with identified causes of growth, necessary stages in commitment and development, and means that will help in directing others to the goal of union with God. The integration of these aspects of spirituality is never complete, for each of the concepts relevant to Christian life is in constant evolution. Notions of perfection, holiness, Christian maturity, and so on, change as our notions of God, person, Church, sacred, and profane develop. Put another way: after our notions of God and Church are purified and demythologized, there is a time lag in popular piety, and only then do Christian lifestyles reflect this new understanding. In addition, our understanding of the human person develops under the influence of psychology, sociology, personal aspirations, and experience, with a comparable time lag in integrating these insights with the gospel, so that we can appropriately adapt our lifestyles.

The relationship between spirituality and Scripture is profound and vital, but it is also complex and delicate. The two are in a constant tension that can lead to renewal or to stagnation in spiritual relevance and growth. Spirituality studies the incarnation of the perennial values of Christian life. To do this, it must have a good grasp of basic sources and teachings and a real feeling and understanding for the development of humankind. It is a broad discipline, for spirituality cuts across other theological disciplines, connecting them in the lived expressions of people's lives. Spirituality, centered in Christ's revelation, expresses itself in concrete Christian existence.

The success of spirituality depends on its ability to integrate the *past* of Jesus with the *today* of the Christian. It tries to bring together the vision and call of the Lord, concretized in changed circumstances, newly incarnated and applied. Moreover, this integration will need to be open to the future, since a necessary tension exists between the possibilities of any spirituality and its inadequate expression in any age. Within New Testament times, we see evidence of this tension and these problems. Spirituality attempts to echo the Bible's call for life in the Spirit, knowing that its call already includes applications and theologizing.

In the Bible we are always dealing with real people in concrete situations who face real choices. We are not presented with biblical spirituality but, rather, with *biblical spiritualities.* In the New Testament we have the challenge of spirituality understood by Matthew for his community, tempted as it is to return to Jamnian Pharisaism. We also read of Mark's call to his persecuted community to a spirituality which emphasizes identification with the suffering Jesus. There is no such thing as *the* New Testament spirituality, and we should avoid the danger of systematizing and harmonizing Christian life. Each individual author has his own spirituality, which is an attempt to apply the message of Jesus to the concrete circumstances of his own church. Our acceptance of the canon of Scripture implies our belief that God is working through the interpretations and applications of each author.

The challenge of Jesus is permanent, but the spiritualities are transitory. As contexts, problems, and experiences change, new lifestyles develop, and when we verify these in the essence of Jesus' call, they become new spiritualities for the Church. All expressions of spirituality must be viewed with reverence, but never absolutized, lest they become a block to our continued interpretation and openness to the biblical call for today. The Scriptures call us to live the unique spirituality of Jesus in the differing circumstances of our world. The spiritualities of the early Church show us how some of the prominent individuals of that time answered the perennial questions of life and God. Within this ongoing religious experience of the Church is a guide to authentic interpretation, but it never frees us from our obligation to reformulate and reincarnate the call of Jesus.

2. Back to the Source

Christianity is a religion rooted in the events and teachings of Jesus. He did not present us with an elaborate systematic spirituality; rather, spirituality comes out of his message. Through the inspiration of the Spirit, the saving events of Jesus' life and ministry are concretized or embodied in Scripture. Scripture is now the Word of God for us, the principal witness of the life and teachings of the Lord. The New Testament texts are the fruit of faith and show the conviction, reflection, remembering, and recelebration of former disciples.

Scripture is more properly understood as a testimony to the Word of God and a prolongation of the word of revelation, rather than as the Word of God or revelation itself. It is certainly not the Word of God for me or for us, since it was written with someone else specifically in mind. Even so, it is true that for every Christian there is an unbreakable bond between the Bible and spirituality. The Bible is the source of spirituality, and all Christian life must be penetrated by its teachings. Life which is uninfluenced by the Scriptures cannot be Christian. However, Christian life is not simply the repetition of what is contained in Scripture. Rather, we reshare, recelebrate, and reincarnate the events we see in the Bible. The New Testament contains creative theological reconstructions of Jesus' teaching. We also meet other disciples who, in their time and circumstances, lived the realities described. Already for us the Bible is a retelling of the events, together with an interpretation of that day.

The Bible, which is the inspired source of our spirituality, and which directs us to the revelation of God, offers us both the events of Jesus' life and their interpretation, adaptation, and application by believers. The Bible is both revelatory and also a witness to humanity's struggle for truth and its search for God. The Bible indeed is charged with life, coming to us in and through the community of believers we call Church. Through the Scriptures we have a life-giving resource for the Church and the Lord's instruction for people everywhere.

We believe the Scriptures are inspired, and that in them God reveals his call to us. They provide the authoritative word that fashions and shapes the Church. However, this authoritative and definitive word is in constant process, for it is a combination of Jesus' message and the New Testament communities' varied interpretations of it. The canon of Scripture is not static but is open to growth. Biblical spirituality, when complemented by the history of spirituality, shows us people who are awed by the holy and live according to Scripture. As we approach the texts we bring presuppositions that often hinder direct access to its challenge and filter its thought.

The Second Vatican Council stresses that revelation is given to the people and belongs to the Church. The Church community actualizes the Word of God through ongoing discernment, which is not individualistic but is a communal openness to the Holy Spirit, that authenticates both the contemporary challenge of the Word and the appropriate contemporary expressions of spirituality.

What is the relationship between the Bible and spirituality? First, *Scripture is a source,* but this could lead to fundamentalism, rigorism, and conservativism, unless there is also the theological task of interpretation. Moreover, the Bible is not the object of our faith but our access to God in Christ. Perhaps before being a source of teachings it is more simply a source of inspiration and edification. We believe in the God of the Bible, not the Bible of God. The latter idolatry of the Bible absolutizes its words, rather than being open to its spirit. But reading the Bible, the believer finds a feeling for faith, a sense of what it means to be Christian, an interior appreciation of Scripture's priorities, and a real resonance of his or her own life with disciples of another time. When read in faith, the Scriptures give us an account of the discovery of God, the discovery of the person's own potentials, and the discovery of a shared mission in the plan of God. In some respects our reading highlights attitudes, not concrete situations, and we discover a biblical mentality or perspective which can then be lived out in new situations, even ones not envisioned by the biblical writers.

Besides being a source of inspiration, *the Bible is,* secondly, *the means for growth in Christian life,* for we believe life must be consciously penetrated by the Bible. We see the importance of foundational events for those believers who experienced them. The Bible is a source of spirituality not because it is the best formulation (it often isn't), but because it is the presentation of foundational events that established humanity's relationship with God in Christ. We see how others tried to be faithful, and what means they used. We read the results of their convictions and faith.

Scripture, however, is more than an inspiration and means. It is, thirdly, *an inspired synthesis and vision* of what discipleship was understood to be. This synthesis is embodied in circumstances different from ours, but the synthesis is clear. However, we require more than the revealed synthesis. After all, Jesus did not elaborate a systematic spirituality; rather, spirituality comes out of his message. His concrete teaching includes authoritative precepts that can be reapplied.

The fourth element of the relationship between the Bible and spirituality is that the former becomes *the occasion for biblical spirituality*. It is the Church's preaching of the Bible which becomes for us the Word of God. Many of today's faithful are victims of the distancing that modern technology has put between them and the Bible. Points of immediate and natural contact between the Bible and people today are now very few and far between, and often the text cannot speak to them any more. As a result, several read their "simple faith" into the text and out of the text. This spiritualizing of the Bible can be devotionally helpful, but it is not being challenged by the biblical text. Such biblical pietism does not generate biblical spirituality. Rather, the text is an occasion for the proclamation of the Word of God, which calls to biblical spirituality. The Word of God is invitation, call, dialogue; it is also symbolic—evoking response; it is sacramental, since it is charged with power.

Fifthly, *the Bible is the measuring rod for authentic spirituality*, the norm and test of all spirituality in the Church. Unfortunately, it is often used as a support for doctrinal positions, whereas it ought to be used as a source to identify the authenticity of present spiritual teaching and practice. All elements of life must be measured by its call. However, there is no prior presupposition of harmony or agreement among the authors of the New Testament regarding spirituality, and thus we cannot consider each individual book normative when taken alone.

Sixthly, the relationship between the Bible and spirituality is one of *constant dialogue* between the unchanging Word and the changing situations of disciples. God, who was already working through the interpretations of the evangelists, is also at work in the ongoing growth of the tradition. Biblical spirituality is only found when the dialogue is mature and ongoing, and we see the echoes of the biblical message in Christian life. Thus, the Bible is the source of teaching, the occasion for new insight, and the confirmation of the teaching. We discover biblical spirituality not so much in the Bible, but rather in people who live the Bible's message.

3. Forward to the Present

Scripture contains the inspiration, ideals, models, patterns, norms, and principles from which biblical spirituality emerges. In our obedience to the Word of God, we see the gospel as the ultimate norm and the common inspiration for every authentic Christian spirituality. However, biblical spirituality is not simply what is contained in the Bible, but the appropriate and discerned application of the Word to one's life, thoughts, actions, and prayer. It is the Word of God in so far as it has been conceived and brought to birth in concrete ever-changing circumstances. Biblical spirituality, therefore, is not found in the Bible, but in people who proclaim it in their lives and in their new incarnation of the Word. This is the essence of both the spirituality and pastoral theology of the preacher. The task is to embody biblical spirituality and proclaim it.

When the proclamation of the Word does not facilitate a transformational change, then we have a Christianity of piety, devotion, dedication, and irrelevancy to contemporary situations and personal growth. Proclamation by word and life shows the significance of Christianity to every generation, culture, and experience, and this is the preacher's awesome task. His or her attitudes must include an interest in Scripture, and a conviction that God's message is relevant to every life. He or she will avail himself or herself of every opportunity to listen to the witness of the Holy Spirit today, so that the Word proclaimed will be the living Word of God in the Church. The preacher must demonstrate humility at the service of the Word, while portraying great joy and abiding peace in the gospel's message.

The preacher does not simply repeat the message, but proclaims it for today. Each time he or she unfolds the Word to people in search of its life-giving value, he or she should be able to say with Isaiah that "Now I'm revealing new things to you, things hidden and unknown to you, created just now, this very moment; of these things you have heard nothing until now, so that you cannot say: 'Oh, yes, I know all this'" (Isa 48:6-7). This newness and vitality in the Word emerges each time it is proclaimed in the new circumstances of every day. Ministers of the Word become ministers of interpretation, or they risk being irrelevant in the essence of their ministry.

There are several stages in the interpretational or hermeneutical task[1] if the emerging spirituality is to be authentic. First there must be a hermeneutics of suspicion towards oneself, one's colleagues, and the New Testament communities that produced these texts. There is a critical need for moral responsibility, self criticism of presuppositions, and honesty regarding one's own approach to the message. This suspicion extends to other scholars in the community of faith to identify their overriding perspective, and it extends equally to the original writers of the biblical texts. This effort to avoid absolutizing anyone's interpretation is part of an initial conversion to biblical criticism which is necessary before any further challenge is possible.

The second stage in identifying the Word's present call and meaning is a hermeneutics of remembrance. Although searching for the meaning of a text, we often end up re-evaluating previous interpretations. This history of understanding shows the living meaning of a text through several generations, and while we want to remember the foundational events, we often remember their critical and spiritual meaning over history— how other disciples discerned the New Testament's call and interpreted it. Seeking what happened, we generally find what was remembered and how it was remembered. This helps us span the gap between recovered meanings and contemporary challenge.

---

1. *See* Elizabeth Schüssler-Fiorenza, "Contemporary Biblical Scholarship: Its Roots, Present Understandings, and Future Directions," *Modern Biblical Scholarship: Its Impacts on Theology and Proclamation*, ed. Francis A. Eigo (Villanova, Pa.: Villanova University Press, 1984).

A hermeneutics of proclamation, the third stage, deals with an analysis of attempts to restate the ancient message in modern terms. The effort to translate "what the text meant" to "what the text means" takes place in the act of interpretation and proclamation. The proclaimer of the Word reactualizes the memory of Jesus—those decisive events that can still touch us in depth. His or her task is to discover the meaning and perpetuate its influence. In obedience to Jesus' words, "Do this in memory of me," he or she tries to actualize the life-giving power of the past in the present moment. In this he or she shares in the Church's principal function, that of interpreting the texts of Scripture. The interpretation is twofold: first it is personal and existential, and secondly it is scientific. This double reading of Scripture is again from the perspective of the spirituality and the pastoral theology of the preacher.

Finally, the meaning of a text needs reflection but also expression in concrete social action based on it. This hermeneutics of actualization shows our fidelity or rebellion to the call of the Word. By reactualizing the Word's challenge, individuals or communities show the living spirit of the Word rather than its dead letter.

Interpretation must be authoritative for spirituality to be authentic. Authority should not be limited to mere authorities, be they clergy, magisterial, or academic, even though it will include their conclusions. It will also incorporate the consensus of the faithful and an inner identification in faith. This challenges each one approaching the text to search for its original meaning and also to see its personal meaning. Interpretation is authentic when rooted in the past and its authoritative Word, when relevant to the present as a renewed lifegiving expression of the Lord's call, and when confirmed by the faithfilled discernment of the community.

4. Open to the Future

As the Christian tradition was passed on, it was modified according to new needs. Perennial values were reverenced but interpreted in transitory forms. The spirituality found in the pages of Scripture already evolved to such a degree that the harmonizing of New Testament spiritualities is impossible. The New Testament communities left the past behind, having accepted it not as a model to be repeated, but as a mirror that reflects the Christians' present identity. Thus, the Scriptures reveal to us our own present and, more especially, our future call, as these texts continue to acquire new meaning.

The exploratory dimension of spirituality preserves its relevance. All interpretations, including the Bible's, are provisional and transitory. Biblical spirituality is closely related to pastoral application, since New Testament writers select from the tradition aspects of Jesus' message applicable to the pastoral situation of the community.

The Bible is our inspiration, it is a means for growth in life, it contains a synthesis of the Christian vision. It is the occasion for new proclamation, a norm for evaluation, and a point of dialogue. It is not a blueprint, but it calls to new life, for it contains insights and patterns formative of a Christian person that we can apply to contemporary issues.

When seen in this way it is clear that the Bible contains and calls forth many spiritualities. In fact, we really do not have a biblical spirituality, but many spiritualities to which the inspiration and teaching of the Word gave birth in New Testament times, and through the Bible and a believing community continue to generate today.

With these foundational chapters on the experience of God in Scripture, the Council's reliance on Scripture, and Christian spirituality's relationship to Scripture, we can turn our attention, more directly, to prayer in the New Testament.

Readings:

Clements, Ronald E. *In Spirit and in Truth: Insights from Biblical Prayers.* Atlanta, Ga.: John Knox Press, 1985.

Doohan, Leonard. *Leisure: a Spiritual Need.* Notre Dame, Ind.: Ave Maria Press, 1990.

Harrington, Wilfrid. *A Cloud of Witnesses.* Wilmington, Del.: Michael Glazier, 1989.

Schüssler-Fiorenza, Elizabeth. ''Contemporary Biblical Scholarship: Its Roots, Present Understandings, and Future

Directions.'' *Modern Biblical Scholarship: Its Impacts on Theology and Proclamation.* Ed. Francis A. Eigo. Villanova, Pa.: Villanova University Press, 1984.

PART II:
MODELS OF
INTERCESSORY PRAYER

CHAPTER FOUR
Jesus and Prayer

Prayer is an attitude common to all religions and in some ways it is possible to view the various religions as corresponding essentially to successive moments in our growing knowledge of God. A natural consequence of this reality is the publication of books and the planning of courses that emphasize the value of yoga, zen, and transcendental meditation techniques as aids to a common manifestation of the religious spirit in prayer. This emphasis is very desirable, good, and valuable. However, while being open to learn from our world history in prayer, it is also important to deepen our awareness from a Christian perspective. With Christianity, we move out of the world of religions into a new world of revelation. Our interest shifts from man and woman searching for God, the divine will and ways to contact God in prayer, to a concern with God who comes in search of man and woman, teaching them the divine will and opening up new approaches to God in prayer.

A further impact on this experience of prayer in recent decades is the theology of the death of God, the secular city debate, and the process of secularization. All these emphasize a philosophical, psychological, or sociological approach to God and a person's prayerful attitudes, concluding in the absolute otherness of God, the gulf of separation between the person and God, the essential unchangeableness of the divine. It results in the need of an approach to the divine which is totally different from that given in revelation.

The first consideration has had the value of opening us to religious methods and techniques that are enriching and beneficial to Christian prayer growth. The second has had a fine purifying result on a less than Christian prayer style which unfortunately had become too common.

However, when it comes to the topic of prayer the revelation of the New Testament may undoubtedly be considered as a definitive stage in the history of prayer, and remains as the basis without which there is no Christian prayer. We discover this profound new insight in various biblical figures and in their focus on intercessory prayer. Jesus himself is the foremost model for us as we pursue the meaning of prayer in the New Testament.

1. Jesus' Own Prayer-Life

Jesus' prayer is a direct result of his incarnation and becomes the culminating sign of Jesus' total submission to his Father's will. It is a concrete way of living his humanity to the full and of carrying out his mission as mediator and redeemer.

Secondly, Jesus' prayer is of revelatory value showing us what God wants for men and women (glorification) and what God wants from men and women (Jesus prays that men and women will glorify and love the Father).

Thirdly, the prayer of Jesus realizes what it shows us. Through it Jesus becomes the perfect ''poor one of Yahweh'' offered to the Father to be filled with divine life. Through it Jesus brings the Father's love as near as possible to men and women. Through his prayer Jesus prays for us, in us, with us. So Jesus' prayer is essential to a full lived humanity and is the guarantee of fidelity to his mission.

2. The Manner of Jesus' Prayer

When the Scriptures speak of Jesus in prayer they describe him as lifting his eyes to heaven (Mark 7:34; John 11:41; 17:1), kneeling (Luke 22:41), prostrating (Matt 26:39), expressing himself with cries and tears (Heb 5:7). Although the whole of his life is prayerful, when he wishes to express his prayerful attitudes in more intense periods of prayer, Jesus withdraws to solitude: the mountain, the desert, the lake.

When these points are taken literally they tell us next to nothing, but within the context of his life and ministry these simple statements already offer definite teaching to us in Jesus' own attitudes. The first group of comments regarding the manner of Jesus' prayer indicate that the whole of personality is involved in prayer with the moment's intensity of feeling. The second, references to place, teach us always to choose those places for prayer which our own experience shows us to be rich in encounter with the divine. Moreover at no time does Scripture state that Jesus prayed in the temple (he taught there). Prayer is not to be restricted, the whole world is the arena of prayer life.

When did Jesus pray? Insofar as prayer is communion with the mystery of God, there are many indications of Jesus' continuous and total union with the Father—a habitual aspect of his life. Insofar as prayer is an opening of oneself to God and an offering of oneself to God, a loving and joyful commitment to the will of the Father, then we must consider prayer as coextensive with life for Jesus. However, there are also clear manifestations of definite periods of time when Jesus more intensely expresses prayerful life attitudes. What are these special times of prayer for Jesus?

At important moments in his own life's mission we see Jesus in prayer: his baptism (Luke 3:12-22), transfiguration (Luke 9:28), Gethsemane (Mark 14:32). This attitude of prayer extends to all major steps in his ministry: the choice of the Twelve (Luke 6:12), before beginning the Galilean ministry (Mark 1:35), Peter's confession (Luke 9:18), before he taught the Our Father (Luke 11:1). Then again we witness Jesus in prayer that Peter's faith will not weaken (Luke 22:31), he is in prayer as he imposes hands (Matt 19:18), and as he shows gratitude to his Father (Matt 11:25; Luke 10:21; John 11:41). Various aspects of prayer emerge; Jesus' requests take shape in terms of his mission and ministry.

When we arrive at the culminating period of Jesus' life, we also arrive at a culminating period in the intensity of prayer expression. The Last Supper, the scene in the garden, and the crucifixion are filled with prayers of petition, resignation, glory, and thanksgiving. In the priestly prayer of the Last Supper, which some would prefer to call the apostolic prayer, we witness Jesus praying for the apostles, for the future apostolic work of his disciples, and for the growth of the community based on his Word. The garden scene presents us with a model of the intensity of petition and the reality of struggle in all prayer growth. The crucifixion shows us glorification and resignation as part of prayer.

However, Jesus does not essentially or exclusively link prayer to special times or special circumstances. Jesus loves to pray simply to express his communion with his Father, to sanctify his name, and to show his own adoration and commitment to the Father's will. Even though a day does not present any definite circumstances, reasons, or times for prayer, Jesus conveys its importance. On these days, filled with evangelizing work (Mark 6:31) and pressing crowds (Mark 1:37), Jesus goes to spend the night in prayer (Luke 3:21; 5:16; 6:12; Matt 14:23; Mark 1:35; 22:14), so important was it to him.

What was Jesus' prayer like? Scripture indicates nothing sentimental or exaggerated about Jesus' prayer (Matt 6:5-7). Jesus' prayer is simple, strong, direct, confident, full of nobility and grandeur. It manifests a perfect filial attitude made up of submission, love, and confidence. In the Sermon on the Mount, we see Jesus' childlike confidence in the Father and his sense of security. He speaks with God as the child speaks to his father. Within the Gethsemane and Calvary accounts, we glimpse the tension in Jesus' prayer. In dialogue with God, he struggles between aversion to the future suffering and submission to the Father's will.

Jesus prays as a child of his tradition with the psalms, prayers, and expressions common to the people of his time (Mark 6:41; 14:26). He prays to God as his Father and opens prayer to an unexpected vision. He prays as the only son of his Father (Matt 11:25; John 11:41), and on this level his prayer reveals the union of his will with that of the Father (Matt 11:25).

In John this unity is so central that Jesus prays out loud, for the benefit of the bystanders' understanding of this relationship (John 11:42).

Moreover, Jesus' prayer is like ours in that it expresses his requests, requests which follow on hope of which they are a translation. What could Jesus hope for or ask for? For himself he asks for glorification (John 17:1-5), not in a selfish way but insofar as this is linked to the Father's own glory. He also asks to be freed from the frightening hour ahead (Mark 14:35-36; Heb 5:7), and for guidance in the choice of the Twelve (Luke 6:12). In regard to others he requests strength for Peter (Luke 22:32), the Spirit's guidance for the growth of the Church (John 14:16), unity for all believers (John 17), and forgiveness for his persecutors (Luke 23:34).

3. Jesus' Teaching on Prayer

Jesus through his life and personal example teaches us much on prayer. However, added to this witness we have the specifically expressed teaching of Jesus on this topic.

The Our Father, the prayer taught by Jesus, found in both Matthew and Luke (Matt 6:9-13; Luke 11:1-4), sums up the characteristics of Christian prayer. It is directed with confidence to the Father and is concerned with the spread of the kingdom and with people's many needs. Read as a formula for prayer it teaches a depth of spiritual expression that is unique in world spirituality.

However, read in another way, the Our Father also clearly indicates the close connection between prayer of request—which it is—and an attitude of commitment to attaining the requests made. Here we see a link between the celebration of prayer and the celebration of life. There is no escapism from reality into prayer, nor is there a seeking of a magical solution in prayer for our own problems. The disciples come to Jesus in Matthew's Gospel and ask "Lord, teach us how to pray." Jesus' reply can naturally be understood as a recommended formula of prayer. When you wish to pray, say this prayer: "Our Father. . . ." However, it is also possible to see in the words of Jesus a group of prayerful life-attitudes—seven in fact, the typical Jewish number for fullness. If you want to dedicate yourself to a completely prayerful life-style, then recognize the fatherhood of God, sanctify his name, spread his kingdom, do his will, acknowledge your daily dependence on him for what you need, forgive debts, and flee from evil.

The Our Father is a prayer formula and a description of the attitudes that lead to a prayerful life-style. There is interplay between prayer expressed and life lived, indicating the necessity of the close connection of the two for the authenticity of either.

A third reflection on the Lord's prayer is to highlight the fact that it is essentially a hope-filled prayer, and in its original form in the tradition it is filled with expectancy of the return of the Lord. It would be unfortunate to limit its applicability to the needs of today. Rather, it should be open to the glory, fulfillment, and meal-gift of the end times.

Jesus' teaching stresses the centrality of the Father in prayer, for this is the heart of his teaching. Recognizing God as Father leads to the loving attitude of one who prays in faith. This centrality of the Father in prayer inspires believers with confidence (Luke 11:13). The God to whom we pray treats us as a loving father deals with his children (Matt 7:7-11; Luke 11:9-13). The certainty of being heard is the source and condition of prayer (Matt 18:19; 21:22; Luke 8:50), particularly in our requests. We pray to our own Father, ''who gives to all freely and ungrudgingly'' (Jas 1:5-8).

Jesus also teaches the necessary attitudes of the believer in prayer. Prayer must be linked to a good life—to justice. Those who ''recite long prayers for appearances' sake'' while living unjustly and exploiting others ''will receive the severest sentence'' (Matt 12:40). The starting point for all is genuine sorrow and humility like the publican in the temple (Luke 18:10). This humble, empty attitude leads us to avoid just piling up words as was common in the caricature of pharisaic piety so strongly criticized by Jesus (Matt 6:7). Rather, the disciple's approach will be one of quiet, withdrawn confidence (Matt 6:6).

This sorrow and humility is an initial expression of faith—a faith that is a pre-requisite for prayer: ''if [one] does not hesitate in his [or her] heart but believes that what he [or she] says will happen, that will be granted" (Mark 11:23; Jas 1:5-8; John 4:50-53; 11:25-45). This initial faith must lead to love and union with Jesus and then, "if you live in me, and my words stay part of you, you may ask what you will—it will be done for you" (John 15:7). The invitation to request lies in the broader attitudes Jesus teaches regarding prayer.

Praying in the name of Jesus is a vital aspect of Christian prayer (John 14:13-14; 16:25-26; 1 John 5:14-15), but it is not a final stage by any means. Difficulties will continue, and so Jesus, anticipating this as a daily occurrence, tells the disciples, "a parable on the necessity of praying always and not losing heart" (Luke 18:1-8). Prayer will need continuous perseverance for growth. Moreover the daily trials will at times develop, for each of us, into moments of major crisis. Jesus lives through this himself and foresees it for us: "Stay awake praying at all times, for the strength to survive all that is going to happen, and to stand with confidence before the Son of Man" (Luke 21:36). Jesus encourages petition in the difficult times in which we live, and this form of prayer underlies much of his own teaching on the subject.

The prayer of Jesus is a profoundly challenging aspect for our own life. Many episodes seem ideal, yet this call to disciples is real, though it may seem overpowering for us. The early Church wanting to live out the challenge was also struck by their weakness and soon deepened their awareness that this Christ-like intense prayer life was possible because of the gift and presence in us of the praying Spirit of Jesus. Without the Spirit, "we cannot even say Jesus is the Lord" (1 Cor 12:3). Just as Jesus at the beginning of his life's work (his baptism) waited for the descent of the Spirit (Luke 3:21), so the Church at the beginning of its life's work (Pentecost) waited for the gift of the Spirit (Acts 1:12-26). Since that time Christians "pray in accordance with the Spirit of God" (Phil 3:3). We are weak, and the challenge of Jesus' prayer-life is great, but "the Spirit comes to help us in our weakness. For when we cannot choose words in order to pray properly, the Spirit . . . expresses our plea in a way that could never be put into words, and God who knows well everything in our hearts knows perfectly well

CHAPTER FIVE
Paul and Prayer

While each of the authentic letters of Paul—namely 1 Thessalonians, Galatians, 1-2 Corinthians, Romans, Philippians, and Philemon—represents different communities and/or occasions, and the remainder of the Pauline correspondence (2 Thessalonians, Colossians, Ephesians, 1-2 Timothy, and Titus) indicate a later period of community life, all the letters are filled with prayers to God offered in the name of Jesus. The language of prayer permeates the writing style in all the letters written by Paul or in his name, whether he extends greetings, offers thanksgiving or exhortations, or shares his concerns or plans for ministry. The letters indicate an approach to life conditioned by prayer and by an awareness of the Lord's activity.

In each letter, we can identify sections on prayer, such as the thanksgiving in 1 Thessalonians (1 Thess 1:2-10; 2:13; 3:9-10). However, the content of these prayers is far more important than their form or placement, and so our emphasis will be on the meaning of prayer itself. Our examination of prayer in Paul will include thanksgiving, blessing, request, attitudes for prayer, and the relationship of prayer to growth.

1. Prayer of Thanksgiving

The earliest New Testament writing begins with a prayer of thanksgiving: "We always thank God for all of you, mentioning you in our prayers. We continually remember before our God and Father your work produced by faith, your labor prompted by love, and your endurance inspired by hope in our Lord Jesus Christ" (1 Thess 1:2-3). The beginning of each of the Pauline letters, with the single exception of Galatians, consists of thanksgiving that reveals something of the situation of the community and gives a preview of the rest of the letter (1 Cor 1:4-9; 2 Cor 1:3-7): "I always thank God for you because of his grace given you in Christ Jesus. For in him you have been enriched in every way—in all your speaking and in all your knowledge—because our testimony about Christ was confirmed in you. Therefore you do not lack any spiritual gift as you eagerly wait for our Lord Jesus Christ to be revealed" (1 Cor 1:4-7).

While a precedent exists for thanksgiving in letter writing from this period, Paul does not rely solely on the patterns in use, but creates his own prayerful thanks to suit his mission as an apostle to the early communities. In Thessalonians, he uses thanksgiving profusely throughout the letter; in Philippians, he sets a joyful tone in an affectionate letter to a community close to his heart. In 1 Corinthians, he identifies their faith enrichment through teachers, preachers, and the gifts of Spirit, and speaks of comfort and hope in his later letters to them. The content of these prayers is primarily thanksgiving to God for the faith of the community and their reception of the gospel message. However, the thanksgiving relates specifically to each community. Paul later develops key elements of his prayer in the main portion of the letter. The prayer uplifts or inspires the community (1 Cor 1:4; 2 Thess 1:3-5; Col 1:3-5), contains a joyful message (Phil 1:3), flows in a movement of praise and blessing (2 Cor 1:3), is stimulated by suffering (2 Cor 1:4-6), includes requests on behalf of the community (1 Cor 1:8, Phlm 6), and challenges the community to grow (Phil 1:9; 1 Thess 3:12).

All the elements of Pauline prayer seem to be contained

in seed in the identifiable thanksgiving section of the letters. In addition, these prayers consistently relate to faith and to the quality of ministry. Paul reserves gratitude for material assistance to other parts of the correspondence, as in the so-called Letters of Thanks in Philippians 4:10-20, where he specifically mentions monetary gifts that the Philippians sent him. The prayer of thanksgiving results from Paul's assessment of the faith life of the local church, and testifies to their living out of the gospel message in the service of others: "Grace and peace to you from God our Father and the Lord Jesus Christ. I thank my God every time I remember you. In all my prayers for all of you, I always pray with joy because of your partnership in the gospel from the first day until now" (Phil 1:2-5). Paul remembers specific dimensions of the community's life, thanking God for "your work produced by faith, your labor prompted by love, and your endurance inspired by hope in our Lord Jesus Christ" (1 Thess 1:3). He commends the Romans: "I thank my God through Jesus Christ for all of you, because your faith is being reported all over the world" (Rom 1:8). Paul also indicates that he derives joy and comfort from the love of Christians (Phlm 7).

The Apostle's prayers of thanksgiving, addressed to God through Jesus Christ, directly relate to aspects of Christian life. Their concreteness challenges us to be specific in our thanks to the Lord, to be truly thankful for the faith we have received, and to express our gratitude for the quality of ministry that should characterize the believing community.

2. Prayers of Blessing

The letters of Paul begin and end with blessings: "Paul, Silas, and Timothy, to the Church of the Thessalonians in God the Father and the Lord Jesus Christ: Grace and peace to you" (1 Thess 1:1); "The grace of our Lord Jesus Christ be with you" (1 Thess 5:28). Benediction is the most stable form of the introductory part of Paul's letters, utilized with almost no variation in all the correspondence. In the opening of the letter the blessing places the hearers in the presence of God, while the closing promises that this presence will continue into the future.

However, the peace wish becomes more than a priestly benediction, particularly at the end of the letter. Paul precedes the blessing by gathering together some of the concerns of the community. This expanded usage is another instance of Paul using a conventional form, the shalom greeting from the Semitic world, for his own theological purposes. In 1 Thessalonians, he calls for holiness of life in preparation for the second coming: "May God himself, the God of peace, sanctify you through and through. May your whole spirit, soul, and body be kept blameless at the coming of our Lord Jesus Christ" (1 Thess 5:23). While bringing concerns to prayer, he states them in positive and invitational terms. Occasionally, Paul precedes the blessing with a warning or challenges the community's response to his preaching: "If anyone does not love the Lord— a curse be on [that one]. Come, O Lord!" (1 Cor 16:22); "Finally, let no one cause me trouble, for I bear on my body the marks of Jesus" (Gal 6:17). In other instances, Paul simply indicates that he shares the world of his readers by offering prayers of requests on their behalf, or challenging them in their faith (2 Cor 13:9; 1 Cor 16:13; Rom 16:19). The prayer of blessing follows the exhortations in the letter, concretizing for the community Paul's understanding of Christian life. It is Paul's desire that the grace and peace of the Lord Jesus Christ be the source of continued growth for the believers.

3. Prayer of Request

In his letter to the Philippians, Paul presents a typical endorsement of the prayer of request: "Do not be anxious about anything, but in everything, by prayer and petition, with thanksgiving, present your requests to God" (Phil 4:6). He also expects that communities will offer such prayers on his behalf: "as you help us by your prayers. Then many will give thanks on our behalf for the gracious favor granted us in answer to the prayers of many" (2 Cor 1:11); "I urge you . . . by our Lord Jesus Christ and by the love of the Spirit, to join me in my struggle by praying to God for me" (Rom 15:30). Underlying any prayer of petition is an awareness of need and also confidence that God will respond to these needs in some way. Paul's personal situation of suffering often leads him to plead with the Lord for relief (2 Cor 12:8), but as a result of his pleading, Paul becomes content with his weakness, since it demonstrates the power of Christ at work in him (2 Cor 12:9-10). The Apostle also attests that the Spirit "expresses our plea" (Rom 8:26), and Christ also stands before God, "and pleads for us" (Rom 8:34). Critical moments open us to a petitionary type of prayer as we, through prayer, draw on the power and strength of the Lord.

Moreover, the prayer of petition goes beyond usual requests for basic needs. In fact, these simple requests are rarely specified in the letters other than his desire for travel to communities (1 Thess 3:10-11; Rom 1:10-11; Phlm 22). Rather, this form of prayer focuses on faith, the quality of Christian life, and effectiveness in ministry.

Prayers of request often speak of the sharing of faith and growth in understanding (Phlm 6). "But what does it matter? The important thing is that in every way, whether from false motives or true, Christ is preached. And because of this I rejoice. Yes, and I will continue to rejoice" (Eph 1:18). Furthermore, Paul prays that their enlightened faith leads to an understanding of God's will (Col 1:9; 2 Thess 1:11-12). The prayer of petition quickly moves in the direction of Christian life, praying that they "lead a life worthy of the Lord, fully pleasing to him, bearing fruit in every good work and increasing in the knowledge of God" (Col 1:10). The quality of life is of major concern to Paul and the content of his request: "And it is my prayer that your love may abound more and more with knowledge and all discernment, so that you may approve what is excellent, and may be pure and blameless for the day of Christ" (Phil 1:9-10). These prayers present a challenge to the community as they identify areas of need.

The greatest number of Paul's prayers of petition direct our attention to ministry: "I urge you . . . by our Lord Jesus Christ and by the love of the Spirit, to join me in my struggle by praying to God for me. Pray that I may be rescued from the unbelievers in Judea and that my service in Jerusalem may be acceptable to the saints there" (Rom 15:30-31). This specific request notes the difficult relationship with the Jerusalem Church, but also Paul's desire for unity. He also sees the community's witness of Christian life as having implications for evangelization: "Now we pray to God that you will not do anything wrong. Not that people will see that we have stood the test but that you will do what is right even though we may seem to have failed" (2 Cor 13:7). This witness requires strength as the writer notes in Ephesians 3:16: "I pray that out of his glorious riches he may strengthen you with power through his Spirit in your inner being." Paul himself needs this strengthening during his own imprisonment, which is an opportunity to proclaim the gospel, and so he suggests: "Pray also for me, that whenever I open my mouth, words may be given me so that I will fearlessly make known the mystery of the gospel" (Eph 6:19-20; *see* Phil 1:19; Col 4:3-4). The prayer of request is often described in terms of struggling (Rom 15:30) and wrestling (Col 4:12), indicating the feeling behind these petitions on behalf of oneself and others. Thus, the prayer of petition becomes a sharpening of one's sense of faith, a statement on the quality of Christian life and a redirection of ministry. These prayers suggest a broadening of our own requests to center on the real values of our Christian existence, thus challenging us to ongoing conversion.

4. Attitudes in Prayer

The various prayer texts in Paul reveal attitudes that the Apostle advocates to all who wish to deepen their relationship with the Lord. Primary among these is Paul's admonition to "pray constantly" (1 Thess 5:17). He reiterates this in many letters: "Do not give up if trials come; keep on praying" (Rom 12:12); "Night and day we pray most earnestly that we may see you again and supply what is lacking in your faith" (1 Thess 3:10); "And pray in the Spirit on all occasions with all kinds of prayers and requests. With this in mind, be alert and always keep on praying for all the saints" (Eph 6:18). "For this reason, since the day we heard about you, we have not stopped praying for you and asking God to fill you with the knowledge of his will through all spiritual wisdom and under-standing'' (Col 1:9).

In addition to constancy and fidelity in prayer, the letters emphasize the importance of time set aside for prayer (1 Cor 7:5) that reflects our devotion to prayer (Col 4:2). Paul himself experiences intense periods of prayer that foster in him a prayer attitude in every moment of life. The challenge to "pray constantly" requires a comparable commitment to intensity of prayer in each believer.

Closely following this recurring admonition is the insight that prayer involves the total person: "For this reason anyone who speaks in a tongue should pray that he [or she] may interpret what he [or she] says. For if I pray in a tongue, my spirit prays, but my mind is unfruitful. So what shall I do? I will pray with my spirit, but I will also pray with my mind; I will sing with my spirit, but I will also sing with my mind" (1 Cor 14:13-15). Likewise, an appropriate attitude in prayer is joy, as Paul suggests in his Philippian correspondence: "In all my prayers for all of you, I always pray with joy" (Phil 1:4; *see* Phil 1:19). Prayer opens us to receive the spiritual blessings of the Lord and to recognize God's gift to us in Jesus Christ (Eph 1:3-6). Our openness to the Lord prepares us to receive the promised Spirit (Col 3:14), allowing us to share effectively in the Spirit's gifts that build up the faith community. Prayer also sensitizes us to our new freedom in Christ and so our lives can be continually directed by the Spirit (Col 5:25).

As Paul nurtures prayerful attitudes in the communities, he also suggests openness to various forms of prayer. But all prayer results in the glory and praise of God (Rom 15:9-11). God's choice of the community calls forth glory and praise (Eph 1:12), and even persecution can lead to blessing for people of faith (1 Cor 4:12). Paul gives other reasons for praise, such as the community's acceptance of one another: "May the God who gives endurance and encouragement give you a spirit of unity among yourselves as you follow Christ Jesus, so that with one heart and mouth you may glorify the God and Father of our Lord Jesus Christ. Accept one another, then, just as Christ accepted you, in order to bring praise to God" (Rom 15:5-7). The expression of Christian principles in the life of the community elicits praise and affirmation on the part of the Apostle, and represents an offering of praise to God.

The attitudes Paul suggests in prayer are basic ones: constancy, totality, joy, openness, and praise. These attitudes underlie the various forms of prayer noted in the letter: prayer of thanksgiving, blessing, petition, as well as the communal forms of faith sharing dealt with in another section. These attitudes directly relate to the situation and needs of particular communities. Again, Paul suggests to us that we cultivate attitudes for prayer that are consistent with our lives, communities, and contemporary experience.

5. Prayer and Christian Growth

Another element surfaces as we examine Paul's approach to prayer, the relationship of prayer to personal and communal growth. While the Lord accepts us as we are, knowing that we are open to transformation, Paul seems consistently to challenge others to grow and to change: ''What I fed you with was milk, not solid food, for you were not ready for it'' (1 Cor 3:2). However, the Corinthians, like ourselves, are to put away the things of a child (1 Cor 13:9-12). With this community Paul also reflects: ''We are glad whenever we are weak but you are strong; and our prayer is for your perfection'' (2 Cor 13:9). The goal of Christian existence is transformation into the image of Jesus Christ (Rom 8:29), and growth in this direction is the substance of most of Paul's exhortations and prayers in the letters.

Prayer for us requires a similar perspective. More than acceptance of our prayer as it is, the Scripture suggests that we open ourselves to growth in prayer. Furthermore, we are to be transformed into the image of Jesus, not to conform the image of Jesus to our present existence. This too is a value as we make our requests in prayer.

The starting point for prayer in Paul's letters is the conviction of God's presence to the human person and the human community, a realization for all who dare to pray. The spirit of prayer that permeates Paul's understanding comes to us in Galatians: ''But when the time had fully come, God sent his Son, born of a woman, born under law, to redeem those under law, that we might receive the full rights of sons [and daughters]. Because you are [children], God sent the Spirit of the Son into our hearts, the Spirit who calls out, 'Abba, Father' '' (Gal 4:4-6; *see* Rom 8:14-16). Romans reiterates this reality adding only that ''as co-heirs with Christ, we share his suffering so as to share his glory'' (Rom 8:17). He also comments later on in this chapter that ''For those God foreknew he also predestined to be conformed to the likeness of the Son, that he might be the firstborn among many'' (Rom 8:29). Paul's prayers are bold, persevering, and confident because they flow from this personal relationship between God and ourselves, a relationship of union. Indeed, Paul prays that we live in union with the mystery of the will of God in his prayers of request.

Because of this deep and abiding relationship, Paul's prayer remains simple, direct, and concrete. However, the content of his prayers consistently relates to faith and ministry. He seems to share the concerns, enthusiasm, and situations of the communities, and challenges them to examine the fruits of prayer reflected in the quality of their Christian life and ministry. Paul is keenly aware that union with another in faith and service complements union with the Lord in prayer. In fact, Paul does not speak exclusively of union with God without challenging the community to grow in its unity as believers. The prayer of union for Paul represents this dual focus, union with God in Christ and union with one another. His prayers and requests consistently flow in this direction.

While we can identify significant kinds of prayer in Paul, perhaps his greatest challenge to us is to reflect the relationship between our faith and our Christian life. Personal growth requires a mature integration between these two components. Thus, Paul forces us to see prayer in its concrete manifestations, while also allowing us to expand our vision of the meaning of transformation into Christ. Perhaps our requests should be in this vein as they were clearly so in the Pauline communities.

CHAPTER SIX
Apostolic Prayer of the Early Church

1. *Spirit, Kingdom, and Prayer*
2. *Prayer of Intercession in Our Own Lives*
3. *Prayer of Request in Ministry*
4. *Intercession in God's Plan*

Paul's first advice in writing to Timothy is that "requests, prayers, intercession, and thanksgiving be made for everyone" (1 Tim 2:1). In our day, prayers of request, petition, and intercession seem to have fallen from favor. Here we consider prayers of request, and especially one type of petitionary prayer, namely apostolic prayer.

Philosophical knowledge of God is a wonderful background for prayer, but knowledge of human growth and development is also essential. Emphasis on the former can lead to an imbalanced view, especially of prayer of intercession. Undoubtedly, there is a great difference between God and us, but any necessary adaptation, as a prelude to encounter, needs to come from God. And this God did, sending the Son to us.

Prayer of intercession is a valid form of prayer, particularly when linked to personal commitment for the attaining of the request made. Then the celebration of prayer is linked to the celebration of life; there is no escapism from reality into prayer, nor is there a seeking of a magical solution in prayer for our own problems. Genuine prayer leads to an inability to do otherwise than lead a life of total commitment for the realization of the requests made. St. Thomas More used to say: ''The things that I pray for, Lord, give me the grace to labor for.'' When approached in this way, our prayer leads to growth and guarantees efficacy. Luke's Gospel presents three main stages of Jesus' ministry—baptism, transfiguration, and Gethsemane—and all three are closely connected with prayer of intercession. Each is linked to prayer, to a wholehearted acceptance of the Father's will, to commitment to the mission given; and then they are rounded off with a heavenly revelation the writer depicts as an answer to prayer.

1. Spirit, Kingdom, and Prayer

Luke gives prayer of intercession more emphasis than at first glance one would think. The word ''to offer petition'' *(proseukomai)* appears eighty-six times in the New Testament, thirty-five times in Luke and Acts (nineteen in Luke). If cognates are included, the word appears fifty-seven times in Lucan material. Moreover, prayer of intercession is closely connected with the Holy Spirit and with the kingdom. Commentators suggest that Spirit, kingdom, and prayer are closely connected at all important moments in the progress of salvation history. The following are major examples: the annunciation, the episode of Zechariah, the birth and baptism of Christ, Peter's confession at Caesarea Philippi, the transfiguration, the sending of the seventy disciples on mission, Jesus' prayer in Gethsemane, the crucifixion, Pentecost, the election of Matthias, the description of the life of the early Church, the election of the seven deacons, the apostles' visit to Samaria, and Paul's farewell to the elders at Miletus. The general thrust of Luke's approach seems to be that in petitionary prayer the believer channels the activity of the Holy Spirit for the spreading of the kingdom. One of the characteristic features of Luke's teaching is his insistence on prayer as a way of tapping the dynamic energy of the Spirit. In other words, prayer complements the Spirit's activity since prayer allows the person of faith to realize the Spirit's abiding presence and power.

Luke presents petitionary prayer as closely connected with the setting up of the kingdom. It is natural, therefore, that once the kingdom is established Luke's view of prayer should change. Sure enough, once we arrive at chapter thirteen of the twenty-eight chapters in Acts the element of prayer in the previous sense disappears because the kingdom is here. After chapter thirteen, the author directs any form of prayer to the success of the work of preachers, such as Peter, Paul, and Barnabas, and to the kingdom's arrival elsewhere. Thus, Luke presents prayer of intercession as apostolic prayer, prayer that is directed to the establishing and spreading of the kingdom through the proclamation of the life and message of Christ.

2. Prayer of Intercession in Our Own Lives

Only the Father offers the gift of new life to individuals in Christ. No matter how much we try, we cannot achieve the conception of new life in others nor can we do much to help in its growth: "No one can come to me," said Jesus, "unless the Father enable him [or her]" (John 6:65). And although Apollos may help in the planting and Paul in the watering, it is God alone who gives increase and growth (1 Cor 3:6).

While human effort is essential, not only for the development of the new life in us but also for its presence and development in others, nevertheless we must have our priorities right. In this context even great activity on our part may be of little value of itself. In fact, there is an important difference between instrumentality and let us call it "apostolic persuasion." The instrumentality could be done by anyone, but it is the prayer of apostolic persuasion that leads the Father to draw someone to Christ. The initiative is always the Father's, but God places the possible apostolic persuasion in the hands of men and women.

The Second Vatican Council seems quite concerned to revive our appreciation of the importance of apostolic prayer, and moves freely from ministry to prayer: "In order to be faithful to the divine command, 'Make disciples of all nations' (Matt 28:14), the Catholic Church must work with all urgency and concern. . . . Hence, the Church earnestly begs of her children that, first of all 'supplications, prayers and intercessions, and thanksgivings be made for all . . . For this is good and agreeable in the sight of God our Savior, who wishes all . . . to be saved and to come to the knowledge of the truth' '' (1 Tim 2:1-4; Religious Liberty, 14). Elsewhere the Council says explicitly that ''it will be the bishop's task to raise up from among his own people . . . souls who will offer prayer . . . with a generous heart for the evangelization of the world'' (Missions, 38). Yet again the members of the Council say that by prayer a community can exercise a true motherhood towards souls who are led to Christ (*see* Priestly Ministry, 6).

Apostolic prayer is something in which all Christians can share. Moreover, as apostolic activity decreases with the passing of years, the apostolic persuasion of prayer can increase. There are two main types of apostolic prayer: the simple prayer of request, and contemplation.

3. Prayer of Request in Ministry

Let us consider, as we did in the last section, a person whom we normally associate not with prayer but with tremendous activity, namely Paul. For Paul, prayer is not only the source of his apostolic work, but feeds his apostolic spirit, prepares him for his apostolic work, accompanies him during it, and even takes the place of his work at times. In his early writings, we see the younger, zealous Paul encouraging the Thessalonians to pray, but as time passes and Paul becomes immersed in his apostolic work, he never moves away from his conviction about the value of apostolic prayer. Later on, his prayer does not decrease; rather, it becomes more forceful. He ends his letter to the Romans with these words ''I urge you . . . by our Lord Jesus Christ and by the love of the Spirit, to join me in my struggle by praying to God for me'' (Rom 15:30). The Revised Standard Version translates the word Paul uses here *(sunagonisasthai)* as ''strive together with me in your prayers,'' and the New English Bible translates it as ''be my allies in the fight; pray to God for me.'' When speaking of prayer Paul often uses with the word ''prayer'' the word ''to fight or wrestle'': I am fighting or wrestling with God for you in prayer. He begins his second chapter of the letter to the Colossians with: "I want you to know how much I am struggling for you and for those at Laodicea," and towards the end of the letter he says, "Epaphras . . . is always wrestling in prayer for you" (Rom 4:12). In both cases the writer is talking about prayer.

This idea of fighting or insisting in prayer is not new in Paul. Already Christ told us of his esteem for the friend who insisted on having bread (Luke 11:5-8), and the widow who insisted on having justice (Luke 18:1). Moreover, the early Church Fathers see Jacob's fight with the angel in a similar light. Clement of Rome in his letter to the Corinthians (no. 2) says, "Day and night you should wrestle on behalf of the [community], and in [God's] mercy and compassion the whole number of [the] elect might be saved."

4. Intercession in God's Plan

Christ and Paul leave us with the impression that God wants us to pray, and pray in such a way that it seems we are almost wrenching our requests from God. Of course, in God's plan we know that it is not so important what we do, but who we are or how we develop ourselves and make ourselves and the Body of Christ more worthy apostolically. However, rather than examine how apostolic prayer works, let us just concentrate on imitating Paul in the apostolic orientation of his prayer. Paul is conscious of being an instrument of the Lord. But his prayer demonstrates that he understands himself as an instrument in the sense that God uses his human characteristics, energy, and will for the development of the mission of the early Church. Because of this insight, we clearly see the person Paul praying and working for the growth of the early Church.

The second type of apostolic prayer is contemplation in which we abandon ourselves to be with God, knowing that after all it is God alone who achieves all true conversion and gives new life. It is the sort of attitude that Christ showed at the Last Supper: "Father . . . I have brought you glory on earth . . . For them I sanctify myself" (John 17:19). Apostolic prayer is powerfully efficacious: "Let each one remember that he [or she] can have an impact on all . . . and contribute to the salvation of the whole world . . . by prayer" (Laity, 16:7).

We often underestimate our worth as partners with God in the dialogue of prayer. Perhaps the true energy in prayer surfaces when we cry out to the Lord in agony, struggle, and helplessness. Only then does weakness become strength.

Ministry and prayer are complementary. The Apostle is contemplative in ministry and apostolic in contemplation. Prayer of intercession is a typical attitude of limited humanity. Some forms of prayer do become escapes and are unreal. However, men and women who experience need are insufficient in themselves, long for life for themselves and for others, and find in intercession a definitely valid form of prayer. This is especially the case when they direct petitions to the growth and development of the kingdom.

Let us pray with confidence and determination and make our own the awareness and conviction that Jesus showed in prayer: "Father, everything is possible for you" (Mark 14:36).

In this section we looked to Jesus, Paul, and the early Church for basic attitudes and teachings on prayer. In each instance, the New Testament offered rich teaching and consistently integrated intercessory prayer within the larger context of life and ministry. We now turn to the particular New Testament communities of the Gospel writers and to their emphasis on prayer, specifically the dimensions of request appropriate to their Churches.

Readings:

Doohan, Helen. *Paul's Vision of Church.* Wilmington, Del.: Michael Glazier, 1989.

Harrington, Wilfrid. *The Bible's Ways of Prayer.* Wilmington, Del.: Michael Glazier, 1980.

_____. *The Jesus Story.* Collegeville, Minn.: The Liturgical Press, 1991.

Thompson, William G. *Paul and His Message for Life's Journey.* New York: Paulist Press, 1986.

Tobin, Thomas J. *The Spirituality of Paul.* Wilmington, Del.: Michael Glazier, 1987.

PART III:
THE GOSPELS' FOCUS ON
PRAYER OF REQUEST

CHAPTER SEVEN
Mark: Praying in Times of Uncertainty

The Gospel of Mark, our earliest written account of the good news of Jesus Christ (Mark 1:1), reflects the urgency of the times. Mark's community experienced persecution under Nero, believed in the relative immediacy of the end (Mark 13), and felt the uncertainty associated with transitions. Written around 70 C.E. for Christians in Rome, this Gospel deals with changing relationships because of the impact of world events, religious tensions, and community development. This group of believers required both reassurance in difficult times as well as an understanding of the place of suffering in their lives. They felt the loss of great leaders, like Peter and Paul, through death. They needed a written gospel that affirmed and challenged their belief.

Simplicity of presentation, vividness of images, and drama of the narrative strike the Gospel reader, along with an appealing portrait of Jesus as a human person. Read quickly, Mark is first and foremost seen as story. Juxtaposed in the account are followers and critics, miracles and suffering, faith and disbelief. Disciples, children, women, the rich young man, a centurion, Pharisees, and crowds become the cast of characters in an enriching narrative. The momentum Mark creates through his writing style may leave us with a sense of dramatic impressions and of superficial responses. However, to have this impression would be to miss the depth of insight in the earliest Gospel. The richness of Mark comes through in his understanding of Jesus and the community, so that Christians see the good news as significant for their uncertain times.

Although Mark's account has comparatively few explicit references to prayer, these passages occur at key points in the Gospel, revealing the prayer of Jesus to us and unfolding teachings that relate to our own life and experience. Mark challenges us to rethink the importance of prayer in lives characterized by change, demands, sacrifice, and service. The biblical references to prayer offer a first glimpse of the gospel teaching, and so in this section, we will examine the individual references to prayer for their characteristics and meaning.

1. Prayer Passages in Mark

Mark's Gospel begins in the wilderness with the call and temptation of Jesus, and the first explicit reference to prayer shows the return of Jesus to the wilderness of the desert. ''Very early in the morning, while it was still dark, Jesus got up, left the house and went off to a solitary place, where he prayed'' (Mark 1:35). Jesus withdraws from the crowds in the midst of his early activity and becomes absorbed in prayer. In this desert experience, Jesus prays alone; for his prayer in Mark is a solitary encounter with God, even though crowds pursue or disciples remain nearby. After the feeding of the five thousand, in the midst of even more intense ministerial activity, Jesus goes off again to pray: ''After leaving them, he went up on a mountainside to pray'' (Mark 6:46). This encounter with God, alone on the mountain, becomes the source of Jesus' strength and of his authority in teaching, preaching, and healing.

During the journey to Jerusalem, the disciples question their effectiveness in ministry: ''After Jesus had gone indoors, his disciples asked him privately, 'Why couldn't we drive [the demon] out?' He replied, 'This kind can come out only by prayer' '' (Mark 9:28-29). Jesus' response that prayer alone would have effected the cure seemed too simple to other

Gospel writers, and so Matthew adds fasting. Mark leaves no doubt that all power is found in God, and that disciples should cease looking to themselves. In responding to the disciples, Jesus leaves little room for human achievement. Furthermore, Jesus explicitly speaks about the temple as a place of prayer: "And as he taught them, he said, 'Is it not written: "My house will be called a house of prayer for all nations"? But you have made it a den of robbers'" (Mark 11:17). This holy place is a place of prayer for all peoples, just as the teaching on prayer is for all. When Mark writes, his community faces worship without the presence of the temple, and so Jesus' teaching applies in a particular way to those who must expand their idea of worship.

Mark continues the Gospel with a few references to attitudes in prayer: "Therefore I tell you, whatever you ask for in prayer, believe that you have received it, and it will be yours" (Mark 11:24). This confident prayer of request expresses the conviction that God gives before we ask. But this passage also spells out the relationship between faith and prayer. Faith seems to precede prayer, being a prerequisite to being heard. In addition, the faith response is only half the requirement: "And when you stand praying, if you hold anything against anyone, forgive him [or her], so that your Father in heaven may forgive you your sins" (Mark 11:25). Forgiveness of one another and cultivation of right relationships with our brothers and sisters become prerequisites for prayer. In a brief statement on prayer in the apocalyptic discourse, we see another request to "Pray that this will not take place in winter" (Mark 13:18). Jesus encourages prayer of request that is active, persevering, and confidently expects an answer.

Within the passion narrative are the final prayer passages in Mark. Jesus engages in the ritual prayer of his people at mealtime, offering a prayer of thanksgiving: "While they were eating, Jesus took bread, gave thanks and broke it, and gave it to his disciples, saying, 'Take it; this is my body.' Then he took the cup, gave thanks and offered it to them, and they all drank from it. 'This is my blood of the covenant, which is poured out for many,' he said to them" (Mark 14:22-24). And again at the conclusion of the supper, he engages in the prayer of his people, a prayer of praise: "When they had sung a hymn, they went out to the Mount of Olives" (Mark 14:26). This event becomes the prelude to another prayer of Jesus in the garden: "They went to a place called Gethsemane, and Jesus said to his disciples, 'Sit here while I pray' " (Mark 14:32). Here, although others are present, Jesus prays alone, as at other times in his ministry. Although Jesus could shield himself from suffering, he chooses to struggle in prayer with what lies before him.

" 'Abba, Father,' he said, 'everything is possible for you. Take this cup from me. Yet not what I will, but what you will' " (Mark 14:36; *see* Rom 8:15; Gal 4:6). Jesus alone uses this unique address, Abba, for God in his prayer of request. This affectionate term connotes a unique filial relationship that does not appear to include his disciples in this early Gospel. For Jesus, Abba speaks of a union of love and eventually of obedience. "Once more he went away and prayed the same thing" (Mark 14:39). Jesus perseveres in prayer, but as he struggles, those around him sleep. In Scripture, the person in distress prays three times (2 Cor 12:8; Dan 6:10-13). Only after this struggle does obedience and acceptance come. Finally, Jesus embraces the path of suffering and death before him, but his disciples, who do not pray, lack the strength for what lies ahead.

The last reference to prayer in the Gospel is the beginning of Psalm 22, spoken by Jesus on the cross: "And at the ninth hour Jesus cried out in a loud voice, *'Eloi, Eloi, lama sabachthani?'*—which means, 'My God, my God, why have you forsaken me?' " (Mark 15:34). Abandoned by his followers, radically alone in death, even God seems absent. Yet Jesus prays "My God" for God is real at all times even though one can feel forsaken. In a loud voice Jesus utters a cry of faith, believing in the presence of God in this moment, although humanly feeling abandoned by all.

While the references to prayer in the Gospel of Mark are not numerous, they occur at key moments in the narrative. Jesus prays at the beginning of his ministry (Mark 1:35), in the midst of intense activity (Mark 6:46), and as he approaches his hour (Mark 14:32-39). During these times Jesus prays alone and at night, symbolizing expectation and tension. His prayer includes thanksgiving, praise, and request. This portrayal is consistent with both Mark's sense of urgency and his focus on suffering.

Jesus addresses God intimately, revealing a personal experience of God. The places of prayer vary, being the wilderness, desert, mountain, table, garden, and cross. The kinds of prayer also seem to vary in Mark, with important teaching presented in these texts. Likewise, Jesus challenges followers to pray both directly and also by his own example of prayer.

2. Characteristics of Prayer in Mark

In the Gospel of Mark, Jesus becomes a model of prayer for his followers. The few instances that Jesus prays in the Gospel reveal that prayer permeates his life and ministry. He is open to the action of God in and through him, even to the point of seeking refuge from the crowds in order to spend time in solitude (Mark 1:35; 6:41). He also withdraws from the disciples to struggle with temptation in Gethsemane (Mark 14:32-42). When the demands of ministry are greatest, and when he needs a clear perspective at the beginning and end of his active ministry, he chooses the opportunity for prayer.

The actual prayer of Jesus reveals the content of his requests and the quality of perseverance, for he prays three times in Gethsemane. In this powerful intercession, Jesus remains open to the Father's will. This prayer is also simple, for Scripture tells us he uses the same prayer again and again. After conscious deliberation in the garden, Jesus' prayer results in obedience.

In a number of passages in Mark, Jesus' prayer is the traditional prayer of his people: the thanksgiving at the meal (Mark 6:41), a hymn of praise while going to the garden (Mark 14:26), and a psalm on the cross (Mark 15:34). After a period of prayer, Mark presents Jesus' ministry as being more effective than before (Mark 6–8). In fact, prayer leads to a greater response of service through teaching and healing. Mark emphasizes balance between withdrawal and involvement. In this Gospel, the human Jesus prays as a person in anguish in the garden and on the cross, with these circumstances testing his faith.

Further teaching on prayer also emerges in Mark's Gospel. Since the focus of all prayer is God, Jesus challenges his followers to cease looking to themselves. All power is found in God. Effectiveness in ministry is the result of being open to the action of God, and not the product of human achievement. The disciples cannot heal, a humanly frustrating experience, because they do not pray. Effectiveness in ministry and prayer are intimately connected throughout this Gospel.

The place of prayer and prayer itself is open to all people. No one has a monopoly on the forms, quality, or places of prayer.

Prayer and faith are linked together, for to pray is the equivalent of an act of faith. The prerequisites for prayer are trust and belief. Confident prayer will be answered, for Mark suggests that we present urgent requests and expect a prompt response. Mark notes efficacious prayer on behalf of others in the episode of the paralytic (Mark 2:1-12) and the Gentile woman's daughter possessed by a demon (Mark 7:24-30). Prayer in this context heightens our awareness of God acting in our lives, so that we see God's loving care in new ways.

Prayer always includes a right relationship with others, and in this sense builds community. Forgiveness and living according to gospel values are essential to prayer. Likewise, an appropriate relationship with God who responds in love is also a condition for prayer.

As we read Mark's Gospel, we notice the legitimacy of the prayer of request. However, we must expect an answer and engage ourselves actively and perseveringly in the prayer. Resignation does not come too soon in Jesus' life; rather, he struggles, grieves, and asserts himself before the Father. So great is his faith that he accepts the Father's will and cries out in faith to God, even in his moment of abandonment on the cross.

In the Gospel of Mark, Jesus is the model of prayer for his ministry, decisions, and obedience to the Father's will result from prayer. His prayer is persevering, draws on the traditions of his people, and leads to acceptance of suffering and death. Mark presents other teachings on prayer as well, by reminding us that prayer requires faith, results in effective ministry, and fosters openness to everyone. Prayer presumes an appropriate relationship with God and others, and always has the quality of perseverance. Keep on praying is the mandate in Mark, a mandate Jesus still offers today.

3. Reflections on Prayer in Mark

Mark's Gospel is a rich source for a biblical understanding of prayer because it focuses on the prayer of Jesus (Mark 1:35; 6:46; 14:32, 36, 39), reflects the prayer of his people (Mark 6:41; 8:6-7; 14:22-24, 26; 15:34), connects prayer with ministerial effectiveness (Mark 7:7; 9:28-29; 11:24), suggests places of prayer (Mark 11:17), and identifies attitudes appropriate to prayer (Mark 11:24-25; 12:45; 13:18). The biblical narrative becomes a starting point for our reflection on the meaning of prayer and enables us to interpret Jesus' message for ourselves and our world. Mark's Gospel suggests the following areas for our personal reflection.

Prayer for Jesus was an integral part of his ministry. Yet it also provided a refuge from the crowds, an opportunity for encounter with God, and a safeguard against overactivity. How essential is prayer to our ministry? What is the quality of our prayer and its fruits? In the midst of demands, can we choose this priority as Jesus did?

The places of prayer are important in Mark: the desert, mountain, garden, cross. A variety of places are settings for divine encounter. In these various settings, we notice that the actual reception of God's action occurs personally and when one is alone. At times, a physical separation from others is important. Do we choose places conducive to prayer while remaining open to an experience of God in all places? Do we focus on the personal aspects of prayer? Do we prepare ourselves for prayer, while realizing it is really God's action in us?

Prayer, as Mark suggests, must be an essential component of our lives, not only related to ministry. Extended periods of prayer lead to sensitivity to the Lord in every moment. Do we give quality time to prayer? How does our prayer relate to other significant moments in life? Do we reflect on our lives, discerning the Lord's action? Does our experience, study, and prayer sensitize us to the deepest realities of life?

Prayer can open us to the deepest realities of life, even to suffering, rather than creating attitudes that shield us from them. We need courage to pray because we will change. Can we, as people of faith, risk the security of our current understanding and be open to new insight through prayer? How do we grow in our acceptance of the Lord's will in moments of prayer?

Prayer in Mark is always the prayer of the human person, experiencing joy, effectiveness, loneliness, and fear. Gethsemane reveals the genuine grief, anguish, and severity of the suffering of Jesus. It also identifies his response of obedience. Rhythms of prayer include peak moments and quiet moments. Every human experience becomes part of our prayer. How does our prayer reflect our own life situations?

Our commitment to prayer and response to the Lord must be lived out despite the contrary values of the world in which we live. Jesus prays while he is surrounded by those who do not understand. How strong is our commitment to prayer? Do we pray when it seems unproductive? Do we choose prayer even when work needs to be done?

Mark strongly suggests that for the person of faith, prayer and encounter occur even when God seems absent or the believer feels forsaken. Our prayer in these circumstances testifies to the reality of God in our lives. What are our criteria for effective prayer? Do we strive more for the experience itself or for the gift of the Lord, whatever it happens to be?

Prayer in the Gospel of Mark challenges us to rethink the meaning of prayer in our lives. How integral is prayer to our ministry? How does prayer challenge our comfort and disturb our notions of what encounter with the Lord is all about? Mark says little about this topic, but in his few references he speaks of the reality of prayer in the Christian experience. As he challenged his own changing community, he continues to probe our consciousness as we live through the personal and ecclesial transitions of our times. Our requests, too, in times of uncertainty, need to be accompanied by a willingness to struggle with issues, so that we can be open to the Father's will, as was Jesus.

post-war years. The Temple was in ruins, and the majority of the Sadducees, Zealots, and Essenes had been killed, leaving religious leadership in the hands of the Pharisees and their scribes. Although Christianity originally appeared to many as no more than a sect within Judaism, a formal break began in the 80s, and by the time Matthew wrote his Gospel, Christians were an independent religion from Judaism. This break was painful for many in Matthew's community, and the resulting tension, debate, open confrontation, and even persecution provoked internal crises for the community. As the Pharisees gained control over Judaism, they revitalized worship in the synagogues, codified the law, and openly confronted Christianity. When many in Matthew's community saw the reconstruction of the religion they had always loved, they were tempted to return to the way things used to be. This led to division in the community, increased conflict and polarization, and signs of hate and mutual betrayal (Matt 10:21; 24:9).

Matthew retells the story of Jesus for his divided community, calling them to reconciliation, unity, and a new sense of identity. He is a skilled pastoral leader, sensitive to his people, appreciative of the goodness of many of the old ways, but open to the new call of God. Like a wise teacher of the law, he "brings out of his storeroom new treasures as well as old" (Matt 13:52). He gathers his material from two major sources, Mark and Q, the latter being an unknown source he shares with Luke. To these he adds unique material from his own source M. Matthew edits all this material, so that it will relevantly challenge his community of converts from Judaism.

Matthew divides his Gospel into five sections, possibly suggesting to his community that he wants them to think of it as a new Pentateuch—the first five books of the Hebrew Bible. Each of Matthew's five sections has two parts, a period of ministry followed by a sermon, the former always exemplifying and anticipating the subject matter of the sermon. The five sermons are Matthean reconstructions, possibly based on ideas originally from Jesus. The Sermon on the Mount (Matt 5–7) is a call to holiness of life; the sermon on mission (Matt 10) is a call to ministry for Matthew's community; the third sermon gathers together the parables to emphasize the nature of life in the kingdom of the Lord (Matt 13); the sermon on the Church (Matt 18) focuses on the challenges in community; and the fifth sermon (Matt 24–25) deals with judgment. These five sermons are arranged in inverted parallelism, with one and five and two and four paralleled, and three as the center sermon on the nature of the kingdom. Thus, Matthew gives his Christians of Jewish origin a new understanding of the kingdom, seeing that it now consists of Jesus' followers. The latter are called to a specific kind of holiness that Jesus teaches in the first sermon. In fact, it is on this that they will be judged, as we see in the fifth sermon. Their life in the kingdom includes both a sense of mission (second sermon) and a dedication to build up the internal life of the community (fourth sermon).

Matthew not only retells the story of Jesus, but offers a theological, pastoral, and spiritual response to his community's need for a new understanding of the present and new directions for the future. He is an outstanding pastoral leader who comes at a critical point in his community's history. He is appreciative of the past and sensitive to those who value it, but he also challenges his people to face up courageously to changed times and new needs. Matthew is one of the prophets, wise people, and teachers that Jesus anticipated his community would need (Matt 23:34). Matthew offers prophetic challenge, wisdom, and teaching that guide his own community through its crises, and he can do the same for us in ours.

2. Matthew's Call to a Life of Prayer

Matthew structures his Gospel in such a way that it demands an attentive, reflective reading. Some authors, focusing on Matthew's use of structure, symmetry, and repetitive devices, suggest he planned his work to be read within the liturgy. Certainly the great sermons like the Sermon on the Mount command reverence. Furthermore, the wonderful account of the infancy narratives, in which Matthew brilliantly parallels each stage in Jesus' birth and childhood with a period of Jewish history, precedes the five books of this Gospel. The ministry concludes with Jesus' self-gift in the passion. Both the introduction and conclusion of the Gospel need prayerful reflection, a sense of mystery, freedom of spirit, and a willingness to let go and be drawn into the awesome events in the Lord's life.

Deepening one's relationship to Jesus is a process of rejecting false values and enthusiastically converting to Jesus. Jesus instructs his disciples to display no showiness (Matt 6:1), anxiety (Matt 6:25), or judgmental attitudes (Matt 7:1); but to control their tongues (Matt 12:36), be on their guard against false teachings (Matt 16:6), and avoid scandal (Matt 18:6). They need to beware of hypocrisy (Matt 23:12), greed and self-indulgence (Matt 23:25), the claims of false Christs (Matt 24:24), and false security (Matt 22:11-12). When their hearts are placed on the right values (Matt 6:21), their confidence in the Father is strong (Matt 7:11), they are willing to enter by the narrow gate (Matt 7:13), build confidently on the words of Jesus (Matt 7:24), and produce good fruits (Matt 7:20). Disciples need not be concerned about small beginnings, since they will be like mustard seed and leaven (Matt 13:31, 33). By carrying the yoke of Jesus (Matt 11:29) and doing the will of the Father (Matt 12:50), disciples welcome the word of God when it is sown in their hearts (Matt 13:23), guarding it like a treasure (Matt 13:44-45). They confess Jesus (Matt 10:32), accept the sovereign will of God (Matt 20:16) and open themselves to the Spirit (Matt 10:20).

Acknowledging Jesus (Matt 16:13) and his awesomeness (Matt 17:1-3), the disciples dedicate themselves in faith (Matt 8:13), detachment (Matt 8:19-22) and mission (Matt 10:5) to grow while living with unbelievers (Matt 13:30). Jesus reminds his disciples that they will need childlike qualities (Matt 11:25), courage in persecution (Matt 10:17), and perseverance (Matt 10:22). Aware that dedication to Jesus has priority over all other relationships (Matt 10:37), they also know that it leads them to build a new relationship with others, as they build up a life of love (Matt 22:37), dedicate themselves to the weightier issues of justice, mercy, and faithfulness (Matt 23:23), and foster solidarity (Matt 18:19) through their correction (Matt 18:15) and limitless forgiveness of others (Matt 18:22). Followers of Jesus yearn to remove need (Matt 25:35-36), feed the spiritually hungry (Matt 14:19), and open the kingdom to others (Matt 23:14). Always ready to share in the sufferings of Christ, they vigilantly await for the Lord's return (Matt 24:42). These many qualities mentioned by Matthew are both the qualities necessary for a prayerful life and the fruits of prayerfulness. They often shape the requests of the community.

The Matthean Jesus directs people's attention to give glory and praise to God. Thus, Jesus says to Satan, "Away from me, Satan! For it is written: 'Worship the Lord your God, and serve him only' " (Matt 4:10). When challenging others to do good, he again focuses on the Father: "Let your light shine before [others], that they may see your good deeds and praise your Father in heaven" (Matt 5:16). After recalling a painful experience of rejection in his ministry, Jesus prays in gratitude to the Father for his plan for the world: "I praise you, Father, Lord of heaven and earth, because you have hidden these things from the wise and learned, and revealed them to little children" (Matt 11:25). Jesus reminds the Pharisees that their teachings ought to facilitate people's encounter with God (Matt 15:9), and likewise challenges the priests to make the Temple into a house of prayer to God (Matt 21:13).

The Matthean Jesus is an example of prayer. The Gospel writer describes Jesus' birth and early life in a context of reflection and worship, even though those initial months are ones of anxiety and threat from enemies. When Jesus first appears to the public, it is for baptism by John, precisely to be an example of holiness of life (Matt 3:15). This dedication leads to a profound religious experience, in which the Spirit fills Jesus, and the Father affirms his messianic ministry. Shortly after this event, Jesus goes into the desert to prepare for his mission in prayer and discernment, and in struggle with the powers of evil. This desert ordeal ends with Jesus' climactic proclamation, "Worship the Lord your God, and serve him only" (Matt 4:10). Matthew's Gospel presents Jesus' teaching as the authentic interpretation of how to worship God, for the Son is the only one who truly knows the Father (Matt 11:27). He goes on to praise the Father for his plan: "I praise you, Father, Lord of heaven and earth, because you have hidden these things from the wise and learned, and revealed them to little children'' (Matt 11:25). Insight into the will of God is attained in the emptiness, helplessness, and dependence of prayer.

In this Gospel, Jesus prayerfully offers his request with simplicity and confidence before the feeding of the five thousand, and after that spectacular event he withdraws to the mountain to be alone in prayer (Matt 14:23). During his ministry, Jesus quickly gains a reputation for his spirit of prayer and his closeness to God. In fact, ''little children were brought to Jesus for him to place his hands on them and pray for them'' (Matt 19:13). When Jesus triumphantly enters Jerusalem at the end of his ministry, his first task is to reestablish the Temple as a place of prayer (Matt 21:13).

However, Jesus' own prayer in Jerusalem focuses on his distressing experience in the garden of Gethsemane (Matt 26:36), where Jesus ''fell with his face to the ground and prayed, 'My Father, if it is possible, may this cup be taken from me. Yet not as I will, but as you will' '' (Matt 26:39). In this time of anguish Jesus expresses his request to God and his need for the supportive prayers of the disciples, but they abandon their prayer and fall asleep (Matt 26:43). As his suffering intensifies, so too does his need of support, but he finds none. His final words are a cry of need, that still express his faith and confidence in his Father (Matt 27:48), to whom Jesus is perseveringly faithful.

3. Prayer and Matthew's Community

Matthew's community was predominantly, although not exclusively, made up of Christians of Jewish origin. They left behind traditions they valued because they felt that their call in Judaism was now heard through the message of Jesus. Matthew needs to build on their fidelity. But he also needs to show how their former dedication could achieve fruitfulness in Christianity, for Jesus is the fulfillment of all their former hopes. What was good in Judaism he brings to perfection, what was not good he corrects. Thus, Matthew consoles his people with the words of Jesus, ''Do not think that I have come to abolish the Law or the Prophets; I have not come to abolish them but to fulfill them'' (Matt 5:17). However, he also needs to let them know that things are clearly different now, and Jesus is the only authoritative source for the teachings and the will of God. Matthew urges his community to build wisely on this secure foundation (Matt 7:24-27).

Matthew calls his community to a conversion (Matt 3:2; 4:17) that will not be burdensome like the call of the Pharisees (Matt 23:4). Jesus can say to his followers, "Come to me, all you who are weary and burdened, and I will give you rest. Take my yoke upon you and learn from me, for I am gentle and humble in heart, and you will find rest for your souls. For my yoke is easy and my burden is light" (Matt 11:28-30).

Matthew contrasts Jewish teachings with Christian interpretations in chapter five, and contrasts Christian piety with prior Jewish practices in chapter six. The latter he condemns as hypocritical, suggesting that the new Christian approach to piety, and prayer in particular, is better. Thus, he condemns the former, "And when you pray, do not be like the hypocrites, for they love to pray standing in the synagogues and on the street corners to be seen by [all]. I tell you the truth, they have received their reward in full" (Matt 6:5). Matthew then goes on to encourage a quiet, confident abandonment to the loving God who knows what we need: "But when you pray, go into your room, close the door and pray to your Father, who is unseen. Then your Father, who sees what is done in secret, will reward you" (Matt 6:6; *see also* 6:32-33). This Christian prayer is very different from that of the faithless pagans: "And when you pray, do not keep on babbling like pagans, for they think they will be heard because of their many words" (Matt 6:7). Matthew suggests different attitudes as we make our requests known to God.

Matthew's community is not only persecuted and pressured from outside, but also polarized internally; as a wise pastoral leader, Matthew knows he has to emphasize reconciliation for his community, and he relates this to prayer: "But I tell you: Love your enemies and pray for those who persecute you" (Matt 5:44). In fact, the Matthean Jesus teaches the community a prayer that includes only one specific pledge from the disciples: "Forgive us our debts, as we also have forgiven our debtors" (Matt 6:12). When Jesus gives his own understanding of a Christian approach to six important teachings of Judaism, Matthew generally makes applications to his community. When Jesus condemns not only murder, but also unkind words, Matthew adds advice, tailor-made for his community: "Therefore, if you are offering your gift at the altar and there remember that your brother [or sister] has something against you, leave your gift there in front of the altar. First go and be reconciled to your brother [or sister]; then come and offer your gift" (Matt 5:23-24).

This community, independent from Judaism, consists of the little ones for whom Jesus prays (Matt 19:13), and to whom he reveals truths hidden from the wise and learned (Matt 11:25). The Lord knows that it is such as these who give praise to God (Matt 21:16). However, the community's struggle-filled efforts to remain faithful are difficult (Matt 26:41), but place the community in direct line with the prophets of old (Matt 5:11-12).

Matthew assures his community that Jesus is the authentic Messiah for which they had hoped. The Rabbis taught that a voice from heaven would confirm the authentic Messiah. At his baptism a heavenly voice does confirm that Jesus is the authentic interpreter of the Law (Matt 3:17). Moreover, Jesus amazes the crowds when they hear him preach and offer authoritative teachings (Matt 7:28-29). Before his final farewell, Jesus returns one more time to his Matthean community, stating that the Father gives him all authority in heaven and on earth (Matt 28:18). Jesus is the only teacher for true believers (Matt 23:8), and religious faith becomes identical with believing in Jesus and entrusting oneself totally to the Lord (Matt 18:6; 7:24). In fact, while the Pharisees speak of yoking themselves to the Law, Jesus says: "Take my yoke upon you and learn from me, for I am gentle and humble in heart, and you will find rest for your souls. For my yoke is easy and my burden is light" (Matt 11:29).

Among the refreshing teachings Jesus gives to the Matthean community are a series on prayer. The holiness of life to which the Sermon on the Mount leads also includes confidence in our intercessory prayer: "Ask and it will be given to you; seek and you will find; knock and the door will be opened to you" (Matt 7:7). The community can have such confidence because Jesus urges them to pray to God as a child prays to his or her Father (Matt 7:11; 6:9-13).

This confidence results from faith as it did for the centurion (Matt 8:5-13), the paralytic (Matt 9:1-8), and a sick woman (Matt 9:20-22). In fact, Jesus powerfully links faith and prayer when he declares, "If you believe, you will receive whatever you ask for in prayer" (Matt 21:22). Faith is the context for any request we offer to God.

Although Jesus leads his followers to new depths of prayer, he also remains observant of the ritual prayers of his people. Thus, he prays before the distribution of the loaves to the five thousand (Matt 14:19) and four thousand (Matt 15:36), on the occasion of his visit to the Temple (Matt 21:13), and during the celebration of the Last Supper (Matt 26:20-30). To his own constant example Jesus adds a saying, both encouraging and awesome: "Again, I tell you that if two of you on earth agree about anything you ask for, it will be done for you by my Father in heaven. For where two or three come together in my name, there am I with them" (Matt 18:19-20). It is certainly encouraging to see the persuasive power of communal prayer. Judaism taught that the community experiences the presence of God *(Shekinah)* when two or three gather to study the Law. Jesus affirms the divine presence to be himself, experienced when disciples gather in prayer.

Matthew writes his Gospel primarily for Christians of Jewish origin. He is sensitive to their love of former ways in religion and can build on those, while pastorally leading his people to new insights. He appreciates the religious traditions of his people and can foster their spirit and correct false practices. He shows how prayer must strengthen them in trial, empower them to love each other, and urge them to build community. He shows Jesus as a model of prayer and a teacher of prayer. As we live in times of religious reform and polarization not unlike Matthew's community's experience, we can learn much from his emphasis on prayer in such changing times. Prayer, particularly prayer of request, summons attitudes and perspectives that enable us to be sensitive to traditions, while remaining open to new interpretations of them.

CHAPTER NINE
Luke: Prayer Permeating Life

The author of the third Gospel is a model of Christian life and one of the greatest spiritual leaders of the early Church. Luke, a Gentile, is a second generation Christian who is not an eyewitness to the events of Jesus' life (Luke 1:2), nor is he a companion of any of the apostles. Rather, he is a convert to the Lord and subsequently places all his life at the Lord's service. Luke is the intellectual of the New Testament writers: he has a thorough knowledge of Greek and writes elegantly, often imitating the Hellenism that he knows so well. Although not a Jew, he knows the Old Testament and in places uses a style reminiscent of the Septuagint, the Greek translation of the Hebrew Bible. He carefully goes over the teachings of the apostles and the early traditions of the Church (Luke 1:3). As a spiritual leader for his community, Luke presents the proclamation rooted in its sources, but he is not enslaved to them. Rather, he redelivers Jesus' message in all its freshness to a new generation. Convinced of the perennial relevance of Jesus' challenging message, he interprets it for changed times, thereby encouraging us to do likewise. Luke's interests and concerns are ours, and we need his attitudes, vision, and dedication as we search for our own contemporary Christian identity and mission.

Luke writes more of the New Testament than anyone. Both his Gospel and the Acts of Apostles were written around 85 to 95 A.D. Unlike Mark, who wrote for a persecuted community in the 60s to 70s, and Matthew, who wrote for Christians of Jewish origin who were suffering persecution from Jews and internal divisions, Luke writes for a community that is neither expecting the end of the world nor undergoing persecution. Rather, they are settling down in peace and prosperity. Living over sixty years after the death of Jesus, the community suffers from mediocrity, lack of leadership, and a need to be challenged to religious renewal. Luke is like a spiritual director as he urges his community to be followers of the way and journey through life in the company of Jesus.

Prayer is a major component of the Christian call and renewal that Luke offers his community. He deals with prayer more frequently than any other evangelist, permeates his writing with an atmosphere of prayer, and uses structural features, such as refrains, to round off sections of his text with the repeated theme of prayer. Luke, often called the enthusiast for Christ, is also the evangelist of prayer.

1. The Third Gospel's Teaching on Prayer

An atmosphere of prayer permeates the infancy narratives. Once Luke concludes the formal introduction to the Gospel, he presents Zechariah, a dedicated priest of the Lord, celebrating his service of the Lord on behalf of "all the assembled worshipers [who] were praying outside" (Luke 1:10). As Zechariah performs his ministry, he experiences the presence of the Lord that at first grips him with fear, but soon calms him with the assurance, "Do not be afraid, Zechariah; your prayer has been heard" (Luke 1:13). The prayer of this devout priest and his wife is for a child, a request which is not only personal but also national, since it implies the hope for a future Messiah. Thus the Gospel opens with the joyful annunciation that the all-powerful God, who is gracious and loving, remembers the people who confidently long for saving grace.

Luke parallels the annunciation to Zechariah concerning the conception of John with the annunciation to Mary concerning the conception of Jesus. Both episodes set the stage for the reverent acceptance of the word of God that Luke encourages in his community. Mary's encounter with God's call follows Luke's typical description of a call to discipleship, with the usual characteristics he considers essential for authentic discipleship: the initiative is God's, producing a conversion, which implies detachment, and leads to ministry. Thus, Mary's religious experience ends with acceptance of the mission with which the Lord entrusts her: " 'I am the Lord's servant,' Mary answered. 'May it be to me as you have said' " (Luke 1:38). The narrative continues in an atmosphere of prayerful reverence; Luke describes Mary's visit to Elizabeth with the use of Old Testament material that presents the visit of the Ark of the Covenant to the house of Obed-edom (2 Sam 6:9-11). This implies that Mary now carries the divine presence (Luke 1:42-45). She also sings the Magnificat, the prayer of Hannah, to praise God's mercy to her and to all humankind.

The spirit of awe and praise of God continues in the description of the birth of John, especially with Zechariah's prayer of the Benedictus. The infancy narratives climax in the wonderful celebration of the birth of Jesus, whom angels praise (Luke 2:14) and shepherds reverence (Luke 2:15-20). The celebration deeply affects those who witness it: "Mary treasured up all these things and pondered them in her heart" (Luke 2:19); "The shepherds returned, glorifying and praising God for all the things they had heard and seen" (Luke 2:20), and when they tell others about their experience, "all who heard it were amazed" (Luke 2:18). When Mary and Joseph, in faithfulness to their own religious traditions, take their son to the Temple to consecrate him to God, the devout Simeon, moved by the Holy Spirit, sings in praise of God's merciful love (Luke 2:29-32). On the same occasion, the prophetess Anna, who spent day and night in the temple in worship and prayer, gives thanks to the Lord for the gift of the child and his redemptive ministry (Luke 2:36-38).

The infancy narrative ends with the story of the twelve year old boy Jesus' visit to the Temple, a story that skillfully anticipates in telescoped form the whole of his future ministry of teaching, conflict, loss to his own, and refinding—his life's work in fidelity to his Father's will.

At about thirty years of age, Jesus begins his public ministry with a religious ritual that for him is a profoundly prayerful experience. In this event, the Holy Spirit anoints Jesus and the Father attests to him (Luke 3:21-22; Acts 10:38). Luke describes it as the start of a new creative period in God's involvment with humankind, and he is the only evangelist to state explicitly that Jesus was praying during this experience.

After this initial experience, Jesus goes into the desert to prepare himself in prayer and reflection for the ministry ahead and to confront the powers of evil, an experience symbolic of the salvation he brings. He then returns to Nazareth, where tradition indicates he begins his preaching. Here, in the local synagogue, he shares with others a new awareness of the direction of his mission and ministry.

Luke divides his Gospel into periods of ministry, and each one begins with a religious experience connected with a new sense of awareness of the will of God. Thus, the Galilean ministry begins with the baptism and its accompanying events, the journey ministry begins with the transfiguration, and the Jerusalem ministry with the episode in the garden of Gethsemane. Not only does each period of Jesus' ministry begin with prayer, but times of withdrawal into prayer punctuate the whole mission.

After a number of healings in Capernaum, "At daybreak Jesus went out to a solitary place" (Luke 4:42). After only a short period of active ministry around the Lake of Gennesaret, Luke can confidently affirm that "Jesus often withdrew to lonely places and prayed" (Luke 5:16). Before the calling of the twelve apostles, Luke tells us, "One of those days Jesus went out to a mountainside to pray, and spent the night praying to God" (Luke 6:12). In fact the disciples seem accustomed to Jesus taking time away to pray (Luke 9:18; 11:1).

Jesus' interventions in people's lives often stimulate them to awe and prayers of praise to God. Thus, we read, "Everyone was amazed and gave praise to God. They were filled with awe" (Luke 5:26; also 7:16; 13:13). After the healing of a blind man Luke adds: "Immediately he received his sight and followed Jesus, praising God. When all the people saw it, they also praised God" (Luke 18:43). As Jesus prayed before the beginning of his Galilean ministry, so we again find him in prayer before the start of his journey ministry, but this time he takes three chosen disciples to share these special moments (Luke 9:28). Later, when the seventy disciples return from the mission, Jesus, evidently thrilled at this new stage in his work, prays aloud in gratitude to the Father for his remarkable plan: "Jesus, full of joy through the Holy Spirit, said, 'I praise you, Father, Lord of heaven and earth, because you have hidden these things from the wise and learned, and revealed them to little children. Yes, Father, for this was your good pleasure' " (Luke 10:21).

During his journey ministry, Jesus teaches his disciples to pray (Luke 11:1-13; 18:1), challenges those he heals to pray in gratitude to their saving Lord (Luke 17:18), and teaches the crowds about the qualities necessary for prayer (Luke 18:9-14). At the conclusion of his journey, he becomes the focal point for the crowd's prayerful praise of God (Luke 19:37-39). Once in Jerusalem, Jesus condemns the lack of prayer in the Temple (Luke 19:46), and in the hearing of the crowd denounces the inauthentic prayer of the Jewish religious leaders (Luke 20:47). Soon their opposition leads to the beginning of the passion, and Jesus intensifies his own prayer (Luke 22:40-44), urging his disciples to do likewise (Luke 21:36; 22:46). He prays for forgiveness for his persecutors (Luke 23:34), a powerful request, and entrusts himself to his Father's love (Luke 23:46).

2. Luke's Special Emphasis on Prayer of Request

In addition to creating a prayerful atmosphere in his Gospel and referring to prayer in Jesus' ministry where no other Gospel writer does so, Luke deals with the theme of prayer more than any other evangelist. The Lucan Jesus is a person of prayer (Luke 5:16; 10:21-22; 22:32, 41-45), whose ministry arouses prayerful attitudes in his audiences (Luke 5:25-26; 7:16; 13:13). Jesus prays before every important decision in his life and ministry (Luke 3:21; 6:12; 9:18, 28; 11:1; 22:41). Moreover, all these references, except the one on Gethsemane, are specific to the third Gospel. Luke's Jesus also teaches prayer, telling his audience to "bless those who curse you, pray for those who mistreat you" (Luke 6:28), to "ask the Lord of the harvest . . . to send out workers into his harvest field" (Luke 10:2), and to "pray that you may be able to escape all that is about to happen" (Luke 21:36).

The journey to Jerusalem (Luke 9:51–19:27), which is Luke's principal model of discipleship, is a carefully edited section where Luke places source material that other evangelists have placed elsewhere. Not only does Luke place material in a different context from others, but he also changes the audience, specifying and directing crucial teachings in this section to disciples and not to the crowds. The journey to Jerusalem becomes a journey toward a deeper understanding of the nature of discipleship, and the teachings become a handbook on discipleship. One of the main issues that Luke inserts in this unit on the nature of authentic discipleship is prayer.

Jesus makes two presentations on the qualities of prayer of request during the journey narrative. The first of these is a small treatise on prayer in three parts: how to pray, the need for persistence in prayer, and confidence in prayer. The disciples understand how important prayer is for Jesus and, seeing him at prayer, they approach with the request, "Lord, teach us to pray, just as John taught his disciples" (Luke 11:1). The result is the "Our Father." Both the context and the shorter version of this prayer in Luke are probably more historically accurate. Although Matthew shows Jesus giving this prayer to the crowds who listen to the Sermon on the Mount, Luke presents Jesus reserving this prayer for his disciples. The prayer stresses the glory and fatherhood of God, hope for the messianic kingdom and its benefits, sorrow, and forgiveness. Jesus tells the disciples that in their prayer they ought to call God "Father," until this point a title original and exclusive to Jesus. Now, the disciples of Jesus share this special and intimate relationship.

Disciples looking to God as Father address two petitions. "Father, hallowed be your name, your kingdom come" (Luke 11:2). The passive form, which generally implies that God is the subject, suggests that disciples acknowledge that the Father sanctifies his own name and spreads his own kingdom. Thus, Jesus' words become both prayer and warning to disciples that their contributions amount to nothing (Luke 17:10). The whole prayer, in the plural throughout, reminds us that prayer must always be communitarian and ecclesial. Disciples pray for three needs of the Church: a share in the bread of tomorrow's eschatological banquet, forgiveness of sins, and protection from the final trial of evil. All three requests refer to the end times and to the life and requirements necessary for participation in the eschatological community. Disciples make only one commitment, "we also forgive everyone who sins against us" (Luke 11:4). Thus, Luke reminds his community that forgiveness and reconciliation are the necessary attitudes in this time of compassion and salvation.

The short parable which follows (Luke 11:5-8), again addressed to the disciples, encourages them to make their simple and confident requests to the Lord with insistence. We find the parable on the friend who needed bread only in Luke. A second short parable, found in the Sermon on the Mount in Matthew, here applies to the disciples (Luke 11:9-13). Introduced with a solemn claim to authority, Jesus urges the disciples to ask and seek continually for what they need. The major teaching is that the disciples should be confident that God will answer their prayers. God's answer to ecclesial prayer is to bestow the Holy Spirit, in Luke the director and guide of the Church's ministry.

The second teaching on prayer for the disciples comes later in the journey (Luke 18:1-8). This parable, again special to Luke, is similar to the previous Lucan parable, except that it focuses on a woman instead of a man—an example of Luke's deliberate strategy of paralleling episodes about men and women. The teaching for disciples in this story is the same as that of the previous parable (Luke 11:5-8); pray at all times with perseverance and insistence. Following this teaching of Jesus is a parable on humility in prayer, very likely told in the presence of the disciples (Luke 18:9-14).

3. Early Communities as Examples of Prayer

The third evangelist continues his emphasis on the importance of prayer in his second volume, the Acts of Apostles, where he urges his community to become a prayerful Church. Early Christians emphasize prayer; in fact, the apostles prize prayer so highly, they reorganize the early Church to give themselves more time for prayer (Acts 6:4). The community leaders are models of prayer. Peter goes to the Temple for the afternoon prayer (Acts 3:1), and later when outside the city, he goes on the roof of the house to pray (Acts 10:9). John also goes to the Temple for the specified times of prayer. Paul, when imprisoned with Silas, spends the night in prayer (Acts 16:25), celebrates the Eucharist in Troas (Acts 20:7), prays with the Ephesian elders before his final departure (Acts 20:36), and visits the Temple in Jerusalem for both ritual prayer (Acts 21:26; 24:18) and personal prayer (Acts 22:17).

Luke also presents the early communities as examples of a worshiping Church. The Church in the upper room "all joined together constantly in prayer" (Acts 1:14), including the communal request for guidance in the election of Judas' successor (Acts 1:24-25). After Pentecost, prayer characterizes the Jerusalem Church (Acts 2:42-45; 4:32-35). Believers in Jesus go to the Temple daily for prayer (Luke 24:52-53; Acts 2:46), pray together in their homes (Acts 4:24-31; 12:12), and in the face of God's merciful designs, easily move to prayer (Acts 11:18). Not only Jerusalem, but Antioch (Acts 13:2-3) and Tyre (Acts 21:5) are prayerful communities.

The special form of community prayer in the early Church is the breaking of bread, which is both the messianic banquet and the recelebration of the Lord's Supper. Christians celebrate this major ritual in their homes (Acts 2:46), and we know that Paul celebrates it in Troas (Acts 20:7-11). For Luke, the community recognizes the presence of Jesus in their midst in the breaking of bread (Luke 24:20-31). It is a time of special prayer and worship.

Luke presents a full tradition of prayer in both his writings and shows how Jesus becomes the teacher and model of prayer for the early Christian communities. Furthermore, the

prayer of request becomes firmly established and directly relates to the quality of life in the Lord. Luke challenges us to
pray as Jesus prays, to pray as a community of believers, and
to allow prayer to permeate our lives. All these dimensions
are particularly important today and provide new breadth to
our prayers of request.

CHAPTER TEN
John: Praying in the Name of Jesus

John's Gospel is very different than the Synoptic Gospels of Matthew, Mark, and Luke. Coming from a church with a tradition unlike those churches based on the traditions of the Twelve, John's community, in the late 90s, cherishes especially its image of Christ as preexistent Lord. From the first line of the Gospel, the reader is drawn into an awe-inspiring presentation of the Word who was with God, the Word who was God, of whom John's community can claim, ''We have seen his glory, the glory of the One and Only, who came from the Father, full of grace and truth'' (John 1:14). The Fourth Gospel gives the impression that it comes from the fruits of reflection and deep prayer; it can hardly be appreciated without a mystical recollection; and it provokes a sense of union between readers and their Lord. While the Synoptics present the faithful with practical directives for moral uprightness and outreach in ministry, John gives no practical directives for daily living. Rather, his approach is to focus on the deepening of one's relationship to the Lord. Thus the Johannine Jesus insists, ''Remain in me, and I will remain in you'' (John 15:4). John's teaching on prayer reflects this relationship.

1. Remain in My Love

The deep relationship of union between Jesus and the disciple is the source of the new life that Jesus brings. As rejection of Jesus means that God's wrath remains on a person (John 3:36; 9:41), so a deep communion with Jesus produces a permanent interpenetration of the believer and the Lord (John 6:56). The former is like a branch that draws its life from the vine (John 15:4), and so Jesus reminds his followers, "Neither can you bear fruit unless you remain in me" (John 15:4). Once the union is broken, the believer becomes "like a branch that is thrown away and withers" (John 15:6).

The union between disciple and Jesus allows the former to ask the Father confidently for the needed blessings of life, knowing that the Father will respond (John 15:7). This union of love and obedience (John 15:9-10), modelled on Jesus' relationship with his Father (John 15:10), is the principal concern of the true disciple. This leads to the rewarding situation described by the evangelist, "From the fullness of his grace we have all received one blessing after another" (John 1:16). On this basic understanding rests John's perspective on prayer and the context for making our prayers known to God.

2. Prayer in the Fourth Gospel

Prayer consists essentially of union with God, and that union produces an external manifestation of one's identification with God. John calls this "glory." His Gospel shows that Jesus rejects the praise of people (John 5:41) and urges others to do likewise (John 5:44). Instead, Jesus prays that the Father may glorify him (John 12:28; 13:32). After saying this, he looked toward heaven and prayed: "Father, the time has come. Glorify your Son, that your Son may glorify you . . . glorify me in your presence with the glory I had with you before the world began" (John 17:1, 5). How exalted is the content of this prayer of request by Jesus!

In the episodes of the interview with the Greeks, the raising of Lazarus, and the final prayer of Jesus, he prays that the Father may glorify him. He does so with great confidence, anticipating the Father's response: "Father, I thank you that you have heard me. I knew that you always hear me, but I said this for the benefit of the people standing here, that they may believe that you sent me" (John 11:41-42). Others, too, have confidence that the Father will hear Jesus (John 11:22). Jesus goes on to assure his followers that they should have similar confidence in him: "I tell you the truth, anyone who has faith in me will do what I have been doing. [That one] will do even greater things than these, because I am going to the Father" (John 14:12).

When Jesus visits Sychar in Samaria, he meets a Samaritan woman who comes to draw water from the well. In the course of an interesting dialogue, during which Jesus tries to tell her all about himself and she tries to tell Jesus nothing about herself, the woman avoids Jesus' challenge by digressing to talk about the Samaritan holy mountain. Jesus then focuses on the authentic nature of prayer in the new age he brings: "Yet a time is coming and has now come when the true worshipers will worship the Father in spirit and truth, for they are the kind of worshipers the Father seeks" (John 4:23). Jesus declares that the spiritual worship of one's heart now replaces the primitive accumulations of rituals and sacrifices: "God is spirit, and . . . worshipers must worship in spirit and in truth" (John 4:24).

The confident request of the royal official on behalf of his sick son exemplifies authentic prayer (John 4:46-54). It is also seen in the self-abandonment to providence by the invalid of thirty-eight years (John 5:1-15). Peter illustrates it when on behalf of the apostles he affirms their unflinching faith in Jesus: "Lord, to whom shall we go? You have the words of eternal life. We believe and know that you are the Holy One of God" (John 6:68-69). The blind man, healed at the pool of Siloam, grows in faith as he courageously resists the sarcasm and criticisms of the Pharisees, and matures to deep faith in Jesus: " 'Lord, I believe,' and he worshiped him" (John 9:38). In John's Gospel, Martha formulates the confession of faith that the Synoptics reserve for Peter, and Jesus responds to her faith-filled prayer (John 11:27).

When materialistic individuals request bread, Jesus tries to move them to a deeper appreciation of the living bread that satisfies all hunger and brings eternal life (John 6:51). Simple requests take on deeper significance. Representing his call to union with his life and love, Jesus again assures the believer of the resulting life of intimacy: "Whoever eats my flesh and drinks my blood remains in me, and I in him. Just as the living Father sent me and I live because of the Father, so the one who feeds on me will live because of me" (John 6:56-57).

Later, Jesus tells his disciples not to be anxious, but to trust in God and trust also in Jesus himself. He then reminds the disciples several times that if they make requests in his name they will be answered (John 14:13-14; 15:16; 16:23, 26). In the prayer of request, trust and confidence play an important role.

3. The Petitionary Prayers of the Johannine Jesus

Jesus is constantly aware of his Father's love for him (John 15:9), their common ministry (John 5:17), deep sharing (John 5:20), and mutual presence (John 14:10). During the Last Supper the evangelist offers us the great prayer of Jesus. Sometimes called the priestly prayer and other times the apostolic prayer of Jesus, it forms part of the final discourses and presents Jesus praying for himself, his disciples, and all believers. The prayer is a superb synthesis of John's Christology, interspersed with instructions to the disciples. Addressed by the risen Lord to the community, it is a prayer for unity, either for the disciples with Jesus, or for John's community with the Great Church of the Synoptic tradition.

Jesus first addresses himself to his Father. His prayers are often made for the benefit of the listeners, since they give insight into the evangelist's portrait of the preexistent Lord. Such is the case here, where the prayer reminds the hearers that the Father gives Jesus authority to grant eternal life to his followers, provided they accept the one he sent, the preexistent Lord. Here as elsewhere, Jesus prays for glory for himself—a profound request.

Jesus directs the main body of the prayer to his Father on behalf of his disciples. As the first part of the prayer summarizes John's Christology, so this second part summarizes his understanding of discipleship. Followers of Jesus obey the word of the Father, acknowledge that Jesus comes from God, and share a life of union with the Father. They choose, because of their faith, life in the new age of Jesus rather than in the world. Jesus prays for them, but not for the world, claiming that the disciples are now truly his and that all he has belongs to the Father. Jesus then prays that the Father will protect the disciples in unity. The community's struggle for unity in times of dialogue and possible disagreement with the Great Church would require a spirituality of reconciling unity.

Jesus' prayer is enlightening and challenging to his followers. In fact, he affirms, "I say these things while I am still in the world, so that they may have the full measure of my joy within them" (John 17:13). Reminding the Father (or is it the listening disciples?) that he faithfully completed his mission, Jesus prays that the Father will protect the disciples in their work and ministry in the evil world. He petitions especially that in all their life and ministry, the truth of the word of God will continue to sanctify them (John 17:17). Jesus ends his prayer in the expression of peaceful, confident, and contemplative self-gift to the Father: "For them I sanctify myself, that they too may be truly sanctified" (John 17:19).

Jesus then extends his prayer for future members of his Church, those who will come to the Lord through the evangelizing work of his close disciples. His request goes beyond his own disciples and even his own times. Again, the prayer is for unity modelled on the union of the Father and Son: "That all of them may be one, Father, just as you are in me and I am in you" (John 17:21). Jesus then pursues this request a step further, seeing the disciples' unity as a sign of his own successful mission: "May they be brought to complete unity to let the world know that you sent me and have loved them even as you have loved me" (John 17:23). Finally, Jesus prays for the eternal union of his disciples with himself and the Father, something he promised to the disciples on several occasions.

The prayer ends as it began, with Jesus reaffirming his fidelity to the mission of his Father, and offering this self-dedication as a petition to the Father for the disciples' growth in love and union. So he prays, "that the love you have for me may be in them and that I myself may be in them" (John

17:26). This request touches the very heart of the Christian message.

4. Praying in the Name of Jesus

The beloved disciple's great conviction regarding Jesus is that "We have seen his glory, the glory of the One and Only, who came from the Father, full of grace and truth" (John 1:14). The disciples do not pray in this Gospel, nor does Jesus teach them to pray. Rather he draws them into an experience of loving obedience and prophetical union with himself, similar to his own intimacy with his Father.

Jesus lives in union with the Father (John 10:30) and urges his disciples to live in union with him (John 15:4). The disciples' union with Jesus guarantees the granting of their prayers to the Father. Their union includes love, obedience, mission, the Father's plan, and Jesus' glory. When they pray to the Father in union with Jesus, they thus appear as the prolongation of Jesus' own life of union with, and fidelity to, the Father. Jesus can confidently affirm, "If you remain in me and my words remain in you, ask whatever you wish, and it will be given you" (John 15:7).

Throughout his ministry Jesus pledged to answer personally any request his disciples made of him (John 14:13-14). At the Last Supper, Jesus tells his disciples not to ask him directly for anything else, but to direct all future prayers of request to the Father in his name (John 16:23-24). In fact, Jesus states explicitly that the Father will grant all requests disciples make in his name precisely because Jesus chooses and appoints them (John 15:16). The Father will grant the requests especially when the disciples bear fruit in Jesus' name (John 16:16). While urging the disciples to pray to the Father in his name, Jesus adds, "In that day you will ask in my name. I am not saying that I will ask the Father on your behalf. No, the Father himself loves you because you have loved me and have believed that I came from God" (John 16:27-28).

In John's Gospel, praying in the name of Jesus means living in union with the entire reality of Jesus' life and mission, and it suggests an identification with, and prolongation of,

Jesus' role in the plan of God: "I tell you the truth, anyone who has faith in me will do what I have been doing. He [or she] will do even greater things than these, because I am going to the Father. And I will do whatever you ask in my name, so that the Son may bring glory to the Father" (John 14:12-13). Thus, the Christian in union with Jesus continues the Lord's work of glorifying the Father.

Abiding in Jesus' love is the ongoing life of the disciple, the source of constant strength and fidelity: "If anyone loves me, [that one] will obey my teaching" (John 14:23). When disciples live in his presence, Jesus promises them that the Father will protect them (John 17:11), guard them from the evil one (John 17:15), consecrate them by means of the truth (John 17:17), and bless those they bring to Jesus through their ministry (John 17:20). All these disciples, who are Jesus' own, receive a transforming gift of new life and actively respond to the gift. Jesus' prayer to the Father for them is "that the love you have for me may be in them and that I myself may be in them" (John 17:26). It is in this intimate union that disciples then appear before the Father praying for the glorification of Jesus through the ongoing success of his mission. Prayer, with its underlying requests, takes on fuller significance in John's Gospel as he places this prayer within the framework of love, glorification, and union. This understanding challenges all of us as Church to be a sign of union and to pray from this perspective.

This section on prayer in the Gospels focused specifically on prayer within the communities of the evangelists. Jesus and his teaching, interpreted for these believers, strike chords that resonate with our needs and search for deeper union and significant life. Many aspects of prayer emerge in these writings, and the prayer of request takes on qualities that refine its image. Now, we turn our attention to the praying Church and its specific manifestations of prayer.

Readings:

Crosby, Michael. *The Spirituality of the Beatitudes.* Maryknoll, N.Y.: Orbis Books, 1982.

Doohan, Leonard. *Mark: Visionary of Early Christianity.* Santa Fe, N.M.: Bear and Co., 1986.

Doohan, Leonard. *Matthew: Spirituality for the 80s and 90s.* Santa Fe, N.M.: Bear and Co., 1985.

Doohan, Leonard. *Luke: The Perennial Spirituality.* Santa Fe, N.M.: Bear and Co., 1985.

Doohan, Leonard. *John: Gospel for a New Age.* Santa Fe, N.M.: Bear and Co., 1988.

Jeremias, Joachim. *The Prayers of Jesus.* Philadelphia: Fortress Press, 1978.

Rhoads, David, and Donald Michie. *Mark as Story.* Philadelphia: Fortress Press, 1982.

PART IV:
THE CHURCH
COMMUNITY'S
LIFE OF PRAYER

CHAPTER ELEVEN
Prayer in Times of Trial

While the New Testament suggests that prayer is integral to life and ministry, the most poignant expressions of prayer often occur when we experience our greatest need. Temptation, suffering, and death can compel us to wrestle with our faith response. As individuals we struggle with difficult situations or passively accept the inevitable. While Scripture offers no easy answer to the perennial question of suffering, it does present to us models of prayer in times of trial. In Mark's Gospel, Jesus is the foremost figure of the suffering servant, but we also see other biblical figures who either approach temptation, like Peter, or who struggle with the demands of ministry, like Paul. Biblical testing often comes in unexpected ways, but it seems to be the culmination of all that has gone before. In the Gethsemane narratives in Mark, Matthew, and Luke, we struggle with the Lord, observe the contrasting attitudes of the disciples and Peter, and learn how to prepare ourselves for the temptations we face. Jesus, the disciples, Peter, and Paul become sources of strength for the minister today, for each challenges us to confront issues of significance or reminds us of the consequences of our failure to do so.

1. Jesus' Testing in Gethsemane

The Synoptic Gospels all record the Gethsemane scene (Mark 14:32-42; Matt 26:36-46; Luke 22:39-46). In the earliest account, Mark precedes the passion narrative with three predictions regarding the fate of the Son of Man: "He then began to teach them that the Son of Man must suffer many things and be rejected by the elders, chief priests, and teachers of the law, and that he must be killed and after three days rise again" (Mark 8:31; *see* 9:31; 10:33-34). Mark follows each of these passion predictions by misunderstanding on the part of the disciples. Jesus' rebuke of Peter, coming as it does after his confession of faith (Mark 8:29-33), indicates that the acceptance of the suffering Messiah is the test of complete faith. Just as the blind man in the preceding episode (Mark 8:22-26) requires two stages of healing in order to see clearly, so too must Peter and the disciples reach beyond the messianic mission of Christ to see the suffering Son of Man. Mark prepares the reader for the ultimate outcome of Jesus' life in Gethsemane and on the cross by these pointed references to suffering.

The Gethsemane episode in Mark reflects two major traditions: Source A (Mark 14:32, 33b, 35, 40, 41, 42a), focusing on the prayer of Jesus and the mystery of the handing over of the Son of Man, and Source B (Mark 14:26b, 33a, 34, 36, 37, 38), dealing with watchfulness and prayer as a preparation for Christian living: "Watch and pray so that you will not fall into temptation. The spirit is willing, but the body is weak" (Mark 14:38). Weaving these traditions together reveals a comprehensive teaching on prayer of request in times of trial for Mark's community suffering through its own difficulties and persecution.

In Mark's account, Jesus does not seem to withdraw from the disciples in the garden, but prays within their hearing: "Sit here while I pray" (Mark 14:32). He distinctly prays three times, interrupted by three encounters with the disciples. The human Jesus is "greatly distressed and troubled," "sorrowful, even to death," and explicitly prays that "if it were possible, the hour might pass from him" (Mark 14:33-35). Jesus confronts temptation, wrestles with the mystery of suffering, offers his request to God, and opens himself to the Father's will: " 'Abba, Father,' he said, 'everything is possible for you. Take this cup from me. Yet not what I will, but what you will' " (Mark 14:36). In this critical moment, Jesus, strengthened by his union with God and his prayer, embraces the hour. The temptation for most of us in the face of suffering or evil is to run away. However, Jesus struggles with "this cup" until his prayer of petition transforms his own approach to the hour.

While Jesus remains with the disciples in Gethsemane, his prayer reflects a solitary encounter with the Father, even isolation from those who surround him. Mark draws out the contrast between the sleep of the disciples and the prayer of Jesus. The cup has little to do with physical pain, but rather it touches the mystery of the Father's will for the Son of Man (Mark 8:31; 9:12, 31; 10:33; 14:21), requiring a different level of faith. Although the hour has arrived, Jesus no longer experiences fear and dread, for his prayer prepares him for the passion.

2. Jesus, Prayer, and the Disciples' Response

The discourse in Gethsemane skillfully turns attention away from Jesus himself about midway through the narrative, and focuses on the disciples. While Jesus changes because of his prayer, the disciples reflect in this instance their consistent attitudes in Mark's Gospel, those of misunderstanding and failure. While Jesus prays intimately to Abba, Father, knowing that all things are possible to God, the disciples fail to watch and pray: "Then he returned to his disciples and found them sleeping: 'Simon,' he said to Peter, 'are you asleep? Could you not keep watch for one hour?' . . . When he came back, he again found them sleeping, because their eyes were heavy. They did not know what to say to him" (Mark 14:37, 40). Jesus' prayer could be instruction and encouragement for his followers, but they lack the watchfulness and persevering prayer that could strengthen them in the days ahead. Jesus struggles and changes; the disciples sleep, losing the opportunity of the moment. While Jesus embraces the Father's will, the disciples lose faith, disperse, and even deny Jesus. However, in the anguish of the garden, Jesus remains the loving shepherd (Mark 14:27), concerned for and supportive of his followers, demonstrating total sacrifice in his time of trial.

This prayer in the garden reveals the commitment of Jesus to the Father's will. His dedication passes the point of service for he embraces the ultimate sacrifice of death. While his prayer is a poignant reminder of acceptance of God's will, it is also the unrestrained prayer of a person in anguish. It is not simply a prayer of petition, praise, or thanksgiving, but a prayer that God's will, no matter how mysterious, be done. After fervent, intense, and prolonged prayer, Jesus accepts what is humanly unacceptable. He endeavors to come to grips with the direction of his life in dialogue with God; he responds positively with mature and absolute faith. Jesus' response is a direct contrast to the lack of faith and hope in the disciples. For them, it is truly the darkness of night, as Mark shows through his imagery of sleep and the disciples' failure later in the narrative.

Jesus' prayer in this episode is also confident prayer, for he knows that all things are possible with God. Yet it is also sacrificial, leading to his willingness to give himself for others. He confronts the disciples in their attitudes, rather than allowing their response to go unnoticed. The disciples will hardly have the energy for their mission if they fail to gain strength through effort and prayer. They are powerless without prayer, a challenge not only to the disciples, but also to Mark's community and the Church today. Only with the Lord's strength will the disciples find stamina in their testing. Just as Jesus intercedes with the Father, he also questions the disciples in terms of their watchfulness and prayer. Perhaps this insight is the greatest one we have regarding Jesus' prayer: that he was willing to wrestle with God's will and so gain strength for living it out. Passive acceptance of the will of God, shown in an acceptance that comes too quickly, is not part of Mark's story of Jesus. He hopes for the same quality of wrestling with issues in the mature faith response of his followers.

This Gethsemane episode occurs between the Eucharistic words at the Last Supper and the arrest of Jesus after his betrayal. The darkness of the hour seems to evolve as the sacrificial moment approaches. Jesus gives what is most precious—his life—so that others might live. Indeed, Jesus' prayer, that led to this acceptance, makes a difference in our understanding of the mystery of suffering and death. Faith suggests that beyond death is life; Jesus' example demonstrates that we can be other-oriented in times of trial. However, we still only touch a small part of this mystery of the Father's will in all our reflections on the Gethsemane episode.

3. The Temptation of Peter

Both Jesus and Peter face the test in Mark's passion narrative. But Peter is emphatic in knowing his response: "Peter declared, 'Even if all fall away, I will not.' . . . Peter insisted emphatically, 'Even if I have to die with you, I will never disown you.' And all the others said the same" (Mark 14:29, 31). However, as we observe in Mark 14:66-72, the readiness to make the sacrifice is not enough. We must courageously live it out. Jesus says to Peter, " 'I tell you the truth,' Jesus answered, 'today—yes, tonight—before the rooster crows twice you yourself will disown me three times' " (Mark 14:30).

As Mark pursues the events of the passion he uses contrast between Jesus and Peter to teach us about the fruits of prayer. Jesus gives his testimony before Pilate by speaking and silence: " 'Are you the king of the Jews?' asked Pilate. 'Yes, it is as you say,' Jesus replied. . . . So again Pilate asked him, 'Aren't you going to answer? See how many things they are accusing you of.' But Jesus still made no reply, and Pilate was amazed" (Mark 15:2, 4-5). The drama unfolds as others mockingly salute Jesus as King of the Jews, and Pilate places this inscription on the cross. Jesus gives moving testimony so that we see the crucifixion in this Gospel as the enthronement of a king (Mark 15:2, 9, 12, 18, 26, 32).

Peter, however, discovers another reality as he is tempted in an incidental, almost trivial, way: "When she saw Peter warming himself, she looked closely at him. 'You also were with that Nazarene, Jesus,' she said. But he denied it. 'I don't know or understand what you're talking about,' he said, and went out into the entryway" (Mark 14:67-68). His response is strong, going beyond the inquiry of the maid of the high priest. In fact, he must then deny his associations with Jesus before a larger group, becoming more emphatic in his disassociation (Mark 14:71-72). Peter's denial reminds us that testimony must be given in every situation, but the strengthening for this night comes only in prayer: "Pray that you may not enter into temptation" (Mark 14:38).

The failure of Peter and the disciples to learn from the prayer of Jesus results in their failure to approach the situation appropriately. Although they were the recipients of teaching regarding the suffering of the Son of Man, the disciples abandon Jesus, and Peter denies him. Their inability to watch and pray with Jesus results in their inability to witness to him in the time of testing. Rather than struggling with temptation, they too readily remove themselves from the situation of distress.

4. Jesus' Death on the Cross

The culmination of the passion narratives' insight into prayer is in the prayer of Jesus from the cross recorded in Mark 15:34, Matthew 27:46, and Luke 23:34 and 46. In Luke's Gospel the prayer of Jesus includes forgiveness of others and the handing over of his spirit to the Father. Only in Mark and Matthew does Jesus utter the opening words of Psalm 22, the prayer of one forsaken by God: "And at the ninth hour Jesus cried out in a loud voice, *'Eloi, Eloi, lama sabachthani?'*—which means, 'My God, my God, why have you forsaken me?' " (Mark 15:34). In his last prayer to God, Jesus acknowledges his own aloneness, abandonment, and anguish. Yet Jesus' prayer reflects not despair, but his faith and hope. Even though God is absent, Jesus acknowledges his faith in God's continued presence, for he calls on "My God." This personal prayer comes at the time of suffering and imminent death. The faith of Jesus in this moment is enough to move the Roman centurion to recognize the suffering Son of Man: "And when the centurion, who stood there in front of Jesus, heard his cry and saw how he died, he said, 'Surely this man was the Son of God!' " (Mark 15:39).

The darkness of this hour truly leads to light, acknowledged at the end of the Gospel by its witness to the continued

presence of the Lord to the community: "But go, tell his disciples and Peter, 'He is going ahead of you into Galilee. There
you will see him, just as he told you' " (Mark 16:7; *see* 14:28).
The culmination of Jesus' testing is his death. However, in this
episode of absolute abandonment, Jesus' faith in God becomes
the model of prayer for us. Times of trial call for the fullness
of faith, apparent in Jesus on the cross but absent in those
closest to him. Prayer of request and openness to the Lord stir
this faith within us.

The model of Jesus' acceptance of the Father's will and his
complete faith in times of severe testing represent Mark's
challenges to his own community. Not only does Mark show
us what prayer is like—persevering, struggling, open, accept-
ing, and faith-filled—but he also identifies the result of a lack
of prayer—abandonment, denial, and inability to deal with
life's temptations. But perhaps Mark is also suggesting that
the real source of strength for his community is not only praying as Jesus did, but living our lives in the presence of Jesus.
"Watch and pray" challenges us to be sensitive to the presence of the Lord in our lives, a presence that is real at all times,
even in our severest trials and sufferings. However, to live in
this presence requires a sense of our own reliance on God. Our
own courage, conviction, and resolve are not enough; the in-
adequacy of Peter's commitment, despite his statement to the
contrary, brings the point clearly to our consciousness.

Today's trials may not be, for most of us, witnessing in
moments of suffering or death as they were for Jesus, Peter,
and the disciples. Rather, they may be more like the trials of
Paul as he carries the burdens of the churches, dealing with
physical trials, discouragement, and rejection. However, the
lessons of Mark's Gospel still offer challenging perspectives
on acceptance of the Father's will in faith, the kind of understanding and acceptance that results from our openness to
grow in prayer and through prayer. Making our requests
known to God in these moments of trial is absolutely essential to our maturing as believers.

CHAPTER TWELVE
The Praying Church

The New Testament writings speak of early Christian communities gathering together for the "breaking of bread" and of their fidelity "to the prayers" (Acts 2:42, 46, 47). We also know of the effectiveness of these prayers of the Church: "After they prayed, the place where they were meeting was shaken. And they were all filled with the Holy Spirit and spoke the word of God boldly" (Acts 4:31). The early Christians not only share a common faith, but they express their beliefs as they gather together for worship and service.

At times, we can question this emphasis on the communal expressions of prayer. Is not prayer a personal encounter with the Lord, and because of this perspective, should we not emphasize the prayer of the individual? While this approach may resonate with the contemporary experience of many, the biblical perspective is quite different. In the earliest New Testament writings, the letters of Paul, the Apostle's emphasis seems to be not on the primacy of the individual but, rather, a clear focus on community. Paul speaks of his missionary endeavors as the founding of churches, not the conversion of individuals (1 Cor 9:1-2; 2 Cor 8:23; 12:12-13; Rom 15:20; 1 Cor 3:6, 10). His letters begin with a greeting to the churches, an emphasis that he maintains throughout the letters, even when he offers his theological reflections and exhortations. The building up of the community, the Church, is his prime concern, and the authentic witness of the community is one of his favorite topics. It is not surprising, then, that Paul focuses on the praying Church more than on the prayer of individuals. He reminds us of why we come together to pray.

When Paul speaks of the Christian community, he describes it as the body of Christ, an expression of his conviction that Christians experience Christ in and through the community itself. If we experience Christ in our midst as we gather together in faith, then an appropriate response is our celebration of this presence of the Lord in various communal expressions. Examples of the praying Church are best seen in the Christian assembly, baptism, the Lord's Supper, and other forms of prayer. The resulting spirituality is one of dedication to the Church, with its strong communal and ministerial direction. The centrality of community life reminds us that as Church we must continually assess how we share basic values within families and local communities, since these expressions of faith testify to our conviction that the Lord calls us into being and reveals himself to us in these gatherings of the faithful.

1. The Christian Assembly

Paul uses the term *ekklesia* to describe the early Christian community. The word is an excellent choice because it refers to the actual assembly of Christians. The Church is not a place set aside for special functions, but exists when the community gathers together as believers. *Ekklesia* connotes a dynamic and social quality about the early Church which they then express more specifically in worship: "What then shall we say? . . . When you come together, everyone has a hymn, or a word of instruction, a revelation, a tongue, or an interpretation. All of these must be done for the strengthening of the Church" (1 Cor 14:26). Paul also says, "I charge you before the Lord to have this letter read to all" (1 Thess 5:27) so that his instruction can complement the contributions of the local members. In these assemblies, the early Christians forge out their identity by the use of language, ritual, and experience. The community celebrates its life in Christ by passing on the traditions given to them, sharing all aspects of life, including ethical discussion, discerning of direction, building up the Church, and worshiping together. Specific rituals, like baptism and the Lord's Supper, create boundaries for the community, developing their unique identity in relation to those outside. The Christian community celebrates its life in Christ, expressing its unity with the Spirit of Christ in each moment of life.

Paul, in fact, uses an unusual term to describe his understanding of a worshiping community—that of spiritual worship: "Therefore, I urge you . . . in view of God's mercy, to offer your bodies as living sacrifices, holy and pleasing to God—this is your spiritual act of worship" (Rom 12:1). The everyday life of Christians is the sphere or context of authentic worship. This point is clear in Paul's explanation of the components of spiritual worship: renewal of mind, authentic relationships, gifts of teaching, service, exhortation, thanksgiving, mercy, genuine love, patience, tribulation, the practice of hospitality, and so on. This description of spiritual worship shows us that Paul includes every aspect of Christian life, and so daily life constitutes an essential component for celebrations of the community. We present "our bodies," ourselves, as a "living sacrifice, holy, and acceptable to God." The gifts of the Spirit, manifested in daily life, bring the fruits of worship to our endeavors, just as we bring all our endeavors to our worship as community.

This realization of spiritual worship in the assembly of Christians is a refreshing insight with many implications. There is no designated holy person or place in this early period of ecclesial life, just as there is no profane area. Rather, all believers, all places, all life can reflect or express the faith of the community. Gift rather than designation is significant; life rather than isolated ritual is important. In our own experience, we attempt to discover both this expansive view of worship and its accompanying dynamic understanding of Church. We can also see the broad base for our prayer and worship. Our lives become both the fabric and the content of our prayer. In fact, the way we live is the single most important dimension we actively contribute to our prayer as Church. Likewise, our requests clearly ought to reflect our life situations.

2. Baptism

Within the assembled community, special celebrations occur to mark key moments in our lives or to heighten our awareness of the mysteries of our faith. Baptism is such a celebration, for it is the sign of the believer's incorporation into Christ and the Christian community. Paul states: "And that is what some of you were. But you were washed, you were sanctified, you were justified in the name of the Lord Jesus Christ and by the Spirit of our God" (1 Cor 6:11), and that we "were all baptized into one body" (1 Cor 12:13). Baptism marks the beginning of the Christian's movement towards Christ and identifies believers as a distinct group. The ritual itself represents a dying and rising with Christ, "taking off" the old human and "putting on" our new life in Christ. Likewise, baptism establishes a union with Christ and with others who share the same faith. Thus, becoming a member of the believing community demands a particular vision and results in specific behavior.

In the Christian Churches baptism is a universally applicable rite, unlike circumcision for the Jews. It therefore elicits language of equality among members of the new community (Gal 3:28; 1 Cor 12:13). This religious vision offers to Gentiles, women, and slaves the possibility of newness of life in all their relationships. Likewise, baptism is an initiation into a religious movement that has a mission. Christians, therefore, called to ministry by their baptism, have the gifts for ministry from the Spirit. Service becomes an integral part of Church identity because of this rite of initiation. Paul challenges the communities to live according to the light, to encourage one another and "build one another up" (1 Thess 5:4-10). Using varieties of gifts and services for the Church is incumbent upon all in the community.

In his treatment of baptism, Paul not only grounds the celebration within the community, but he also indicates the effects of this prayerful incorporation into the community. Baptism into Christ becomes the starting point for Christian ministry. Faith expresses itself in mission; the fruits of this prayer of the community result in service. This insight into the rite of initiation suggests that we emphasize the communal aspects of celebration. But even more, it directs us to the fruits of prayer that are clearly visible in our lives. However, even these expressions of our faith commitment are part of the community's witness to its new life in Christ, rather than simply the dedication of an individual.

3. The Lord's Supper

The early Christian community gathers together to share a meal and to remember the Lord Jesus: "And when he had given thanks, he broke it and said, 'This is my body given for you; do this in remembrance of me. . . . This cup is the new covenant in my blood; do this, whenever you drink it, in remembrance of me.' For whenever you eat this bread and drink this cup, you proclaim the Lord's death until he comes" (1 Cor 11:24, 26). This ritual celebration reminds believers of the meal shared by Jesus and his disciples, "on the night when he was betrayed" (1 Cor 11:23). However, it takes on greater importance as the community comes to grips with the meaning of suffering and death.

Paul presents his treatment of the Eucharist with startling realism, as he inserts the Eucharistic prayer into a section of 1 Corinthians 11-14. Unity and solidarity are Paul's themes as he addresses issues of women and men, divisions in the community, abuses surrounding the meal, gifts within the community, working together as the body of Christ, and responsibility in the Church. Paul inserts this prayer well within the life of the community, for an authentic Christian life prepares Christians to celebrate at the table of the Lord. Unity among the group and deep relationships are prerequisites for the Church to be a sign of its union with Christ in this prayerful gathering. Requests can be seen within this context.

The celebration of the Lord's Supper reveals participation in Christ, and all members share in this liturgical prayer according to gift. Women pray, prophesy, and exercise liturgical leadership, since ministry results from baptism and gift of the Spirit (1 Cor 11:5). Sexual restraints have no place in this early prayer of the community.

How the Church celebrates is the major sign for the community of its union with Christ. But Paul links this celebration, as he does all his prayers of the Church, with Christian life and ministry. Worship is never an isolated event, but Paul realistically places it within the community's life, a life in constant need of transformation. This change we pray for; this we celebrate. The sharing of a meal is the concrete occasion for mutual communion and service, as gathered believers realize Christ's real presence among them.

Worship is an integral part of Christian life, and Paul's understanding stimulates our prayer in life as well as in the Eucharistic celebration. Our requests for more authentic Christian responses in daily life prepare us for our communal worship. Today, as in the early Church, Paul's realistic portrayal of this cornerstone of Christian worship reminds us of our preparation for the Eucharistic celebration. Today, as in the early Church, liturgical leadership in the faith community may be most effectively exercised by those who have the gifts from the Lord. Discerning the presence and use of these gifts is part of the responsibility of each community. Paul's teaching on the Lord's Supper concerns all these areas of worship with only the sketchiest outline of the ritual itself. Perhaps we pay undue attention to form rather than to substance in our liturgical celebrations.

4. The Sharing of Prayer

The community also shares its common faith through many expressions of prayer. Paul uses prayer of petition consistently and effectively: "What we pray for is your improvement" (2 Cor 13:9); "You also must help us by prayer, so that many will give thanks on our behalf for the blessing granted us in answer to many prayers" (2 Cor 1:11). He urges the community, "let your requests be made known to God" in "prayer and supplication, with thanksgiving" (Phil 4:6). He also gives "thanks to God" for the community, "mentioning you in our prayers" (1 Thess 1:2), "always in every prayer of mine . . . making my prayer with joy" (Phil 1:4). Frequently, Paul anticipates his later exhortations to the community in his prayers. He prays for what he commits himself to work toward with his congregation, linking request and commitment. We also see prayer among the co-workers that creates bonds of unity and enhances ministry; constant prayer constitutes a value for the community of faith. Not only do the letters begin and end with benediction, but a prayerful Apostle contemplates his experience in the churches and his own call, sharing the fruits of his reflection and prayer with the churches. Co-workers, in prayer, share their faith vision of Christian life, and then resolve to share in the mission of spreading the gospel.

The majority of the examples of prayer in Paul occur in the Christian community. As Christians assemble together they pray: "So with yourselves; since you are eager for the manifestations of the Spirit, strive to excel in building up the Church . . . pray for the power to interpret . . . pray with one mind . . . sing with the spirit . . . let all things be done for edification" (1 Cor 14:12–15:26). These regular Christian meetings include prayer, exhortations, readings, and homilies that assist in the transmission of the religious tradition.

Praying together is a key element for building up the community and for testing spirits. The quality of communal prayer becomes an indicator of the group's ability to grow as the body of Christ. In Paul's letters, we glimpse a praying Church that gathers together, celebrates baptism and the Lord's Supper, and engages in a variety of prayer forms. In all these examples of a Church at prayer we see prayer closely related to Christian life and ministry and its requests along the same lines. This holistic approach to life is a wonderful reminder to us of how integrated our lives can be if we reflect on the early New Testament message. These examples also indicate a different spirituality for our own times, a spirituality that has as a main characteristic dedication to Church and as Church.

5. Spirituality of Ecclesial Dedication

Paul's strong emphasis on the praying Church and community life leads to the realization that his spirituality is more ecclesial than individualistic. Maturity in faith results more from sharing in the life of the Church than from individual acts of piety. For Paul, the Christians' response to the Lord results in a spirituality of ecclesial living. Being Church is the primary commitment for disciples for it is a concrete expression of faith. "Finally, brothers [and sisters], we instructed you how to live in order to please God, as in fact you are living. Now we ask you and urge you in the Lord Jesus to do this more and more" (1 Thess 4:1).

Spirituality also means holiness of life for believers in Jesus. Holiness is God's gift to all, and holiness becomes a reality in our own life situations, since all share the spirit of Christ: "Give thanks in all circumstances, for this is God's will for you in Christ Jesus" (1 Thess 5:18); "So whether you eat or drink or whatever you do, do it all for the glory of God" (1 Cor 10:31).

Within Paul's development of spirituality, he focuses on the components usually associated with an integration of perennial values into our personal lives: "Not that we are competent in ourselves to claim anything for ourselves, but our competence comes from God" (2 Cor 3:5); "And we know that in all things God works for the good of those who love him, who have been called according to his purpose" (Rom 8:28). God is the ultimate source of our life and convictions, and so a relationship with God is fundamental to any expression of spirituality. Understanding the Lord's call to us results from openness and dialogue, the attitudes of prayer.

The Christian dimension of spirituality emerges from the realization that God most clearly reveals the divine self in Christ. The person Jesus is central to Paul's preaching and teaching: "I always thank God for you because of his grace given you in Christ Jesus" (1 Cor 1:4); "For we do not preach ourselves, but Jesus Christ as Lord, and ourselves as your servants for Jesus' sake" (2 Cor 4:5). Paul invites Christians to conform to the pattern of Christ's life for the centrality of Christ and union with him is the basis of the new existence. The Church itself is the community of believers constituted in the Spirit around the cornerstone of their faith in Christ. Thus, Paul can rightly say, "now you together are Christ's body" (1 Cor 12:27). We live out this vision of Church daily, and thus we become more truly the body of Christ.

While Paul's spirituality of ecclesial dedication has many practical implications regarding Christian life, it also emphasizes our own service as Church. Union with Christ is union with the mission of Christ. Following the pattern of Christ, life includes a realization of our dying and rising with him, often seen in the service of others. Ministry is the shared responsibility of the Church and an essential dimension of ecclesial dedication. Again, the fruits of a relationship with the Lord find concrete expression in the quality and diversity of our ministry as Church.

A final implication of Paul's focus on Church is his challenge to believers to instill an ecclesial consciousness in others. Empowering others to live as Church is the work of all believers. Recognizing and offering gifts, creating opportunities for service, sharing reflections on a vision of Church, or collaborating with others as partners in Christ are all possible ways of empowerment that Paul suggests we do consistently. "Never be lacking in zeal, but keep your spiritual fervor, serving the Lord" (Rom 12:11). These areas also form the content of our requests to the Lord.

Paul's approach to spirituality suggests that we examine our own emphasis. Is our focus on our individual growth in union with the Lord, or do we emphasize our growth in the Lord in union with others? Is our spirituality ecclesial? Does it express itself in service of others, and enable them truly to live as Church?

While all the New Testament writings witness to the reality of a praying Church, the earliest letters of Paul demonstrate this emphasis in the Church's life from the beginning. Within twenty years of the death and resurrection of Jesus, the community gathers in his name, celebrates initiation rites and a Eucharistic meal, and uses a variety of ways to share its faith life through prayer. At this early date, we also perceive a unique approach to spirituality with its prime focus on our growth as Church. Requests and exhortations emphasize this perspective.

The Church at prayer insures the authenticity of its vision, for it opens itself to the Spirit of the Lord for guidance in its life. The Church at prayer insures growth as community, for as we gather to pray we share our faith and our Christian lives. The Church at prayer insures effective ministry within the community, for we cannot simply emphasize the prayer itself. The biblical model also leads us to reflect on our response to the Lord's gifts in service.

The praying Church is, then, a union with the Lord and with each other that results in ministry, insuring our growth as community. The praying Church in Paul offers us concrete ideas to expand our views of spirituality and ecclesial life. Our prayer of request should open us more fully to this ecclesial dimension of Christian life.

CHAPTER THIRTEEN
The Eucharist:
The Prayer of the Community

It always strikes me as odd and greatly surprises me that the evangelist who tells us of the wedding at Cana, the feeding of the five thousand, the bread of life, the Lamb, the unbroken bones, and the pierced side—all events with Eucharistic symbolism—only this one evangelist omits within Jesus' last meal the explicit mention of the institution of the Eucharist. That John gives us the institution elsewhere is true, but, obviously, its explicit omission here is not without very good reason. John tells us more about the importance of Eucharist in a community's spiritual growth by the omission here of its institution than he would teach us by its inclusion.

In the Synoptics we read how the last meal develops until, at a culminating moment, Jesus takes bread and wine, blesses and shares it, saying, ''this is my body, this is my blood; do this in remembrance of me'' (Mark 14:22-24; Matt 26:26-28; Luke 22:19-20). In John we read how the last meal progresses until, at a culminating moment, Jesus takes a towel and water, washes his disciples' feet and, on returning to table, says ''copy what I have done to you" (John 13:15). John places the incident of the washing of the feet in the very heart of the meal and ends this incident with a command to repeat it, just as the Synoptic writers have this command after the institution.

1. A Deliberate Modification

This deliberate change of the natural flow of the meal story is very enlightening regarding the place of the Eucharist in spiritual life. Only something important could have led the author to modify the story in this way. He takes out the very heart of the meal story and inserts this other episode—why?

Before answering the question "Why?" it would be useful to ask whether the washing of the feet actually took place. It would seem more correct, in order to put things in perspective, to underline the fact that the "washing of the feet" took place in every Jewish home that night. It was a very simple act of service. As guests arrived for the meal, there would be a bowl of water near the entrance. When people came in from the dry, dirty roads of Jerusalem it was a pleasant, welcoming sign of concern that guests could stand in the water at the door with their sandals on. This was refreshing—a first sign of welcome to the home—a simple gesture of concern, kindness, friendship. The omission of this gesture of concern on another occasion does not go unnoticed by Jesus, and he explicitly tells Simon the Pharisee how he feels (Luke 7:36-50). The washing of the feet is a very simple act that says, "make yourself at home; you are welcome." Our nearest equivalent nowadays would be a handshake.

It was such a simple gesture which seemed to speak powerfully to John of what the Eucharist means in life. Thus, it seems that he transfers the event from the entrance, before the meal, to the period of institution when the essence of the meal is described.

To grasp the full value of the episode we need to bring to mind the few moments which Jesus passes in discussion with Peter. The latter, having refused and then later reluctantly accepted to have his feet washed, is told: "At the moment you do not know what I am doing, but later you will understand"

(John 13:7). Only future events will bring to light the full significance of a simple gesture of concern and love. In fact, it is this ordinary act of love which is actually telling us what the future will be. This simple gesture is in truth a prophecy in act.

2. Prophecy in Act

The Jews were well accustomed to prophecy—not only in speech but also in actions. Ezekiel acted out the exile and banishment of the Jews in the mime of the emigrant (Ezek 12). He lived out the same prophecy with the episode of the shaved hair (Ezek 5). Jeremiah, by shattering the earthenware jug, prophesied the destruction of Israel (Jer 19). The entire life of the prophet Hosea—his marriage to a prostitute and the names of his three children—is one long prophecy acted out for the people. In the New Testament, we read how the prophet Agabus from Judaea arrived at Caesarea a few days after Paul had arrived on his way back to Jerusalem. Agabus foretold Paul's imprisonment by taking Paul's girdle and tying himself in it. He acted out the prophecy. In each case, only future events would bring to light the full significance of the prophet's action. Each time the prophet explicitly indicates that the simple gesture is of future value.

This is Jesus' attitude during the passover meal: he acts out a prophecy of his future life. Instead of just saying to the apostles, "my future life, no matter how short, will be completely given for you all in love, service, concern, and friendship," he acts this out. He performs a simple gesture of love and friendship and service, and then adds, "at the moment you do not know what I am doing, but later you will understand." The ordinary gesture directs us to the future; it is a prophecy in act. Then Jesus says, "I have given you an example so that you may copy what I have done" (John 13:15), and returning to table he adds, "Now that you know this, happiness will be yours if you behave accordingly" (John 13:17).

Possibly a little reflection on this account of Jesus' last meal can help to make of Eucharist what the Second Vatican Council urges that it become in our lives: "No Christian community can be built up unless it has its basis and center in the celebration of the most Holy Eucharist. Here therefore all education in the spirit of community must originate'' (Priests, 6). The Council's major document states that ''the Eucharistic sacrifice . . . is the fount and apex of the whole Christian life'' (Church, 3:2). It continues, ''Truly partaking of the body of the Lord in the breaking of the Eucharistic bread, we are taken up into communion with him and with one another'' (Church, 7:3).

The way John presents the Eucharistic meal complements the presentation of other New Testament writers. Some may emphasize the real presence, the sacrificial aspect or the dimension of meal in their narratives. With this account, John underlines the fact that the Eucharist is an occasion when, coming together in faith and love, we, by the very fact of our presence and participation, already symbolize a unity that exists (Church, 3:2). As we share in a salvific event, we mutually pledge that the simple gestures of love and service we show by participation at the same table, kiss of peace, and signs of friendship, are prophetic of a future life consecrated to an intensified living of love, friendship, concern, and kindness.

Around the Eucharistic table, true love and friendship must already exist or else we know that we must leave our gift at one side and seek reconciliation. The Eucharistic celebration is a celebration of Christian love by the believing community. It already manifests genuine love, is a celebration of Christian community love, and is also a challenge to future intensification of mutual love.

3. Living Out the Prophecy

In the Eucharist, we are not dealing purely with a social event in which we express unity and listen to promises of intensified union. Christians profess belief that the sacraments are efficacious in what they symbolize. Clearly, baptism is a symbol of washing and cleansing. We believe it is efficacious in a spiritual cleansing. The Eucharist is the starting point for all education in group or community living (Priests, 6), and the sacrament expresses the unity of the group in Christ (Church, 3:2). The celebration, however, is more than this for us. Its sign value is along the lines of unity and friendship. Its prophetic value challenges us to intensify our efforts in community life. But we believe that the Eucharist is efficacious in what it symbolizes. We believe that unity is not only expressed but the power of Christ active in the sacrament actually brings about this unity (Church, 3:2).

The Eucharist is for us, as it was for Christ, an occasion when we gather with other people of the same beliefs and hopes and celebrate with them for the glory of the Father an agapé, or meal of friendship. During this meal, our simple gestures of love, concern, friendship, and service are necessary for the authenticity of the celebration, but they are also prophetic regarding the lifestyle to which we commit ourselves: one of intensified service in the future. When the presider says, "Go, the Mass is ended," we know in our own hearts that it is just beginning, and that we must now live out the prophecy. However, we are not alone in our expressions of service, for the grace of the sacrament consists in the efficacious assistance of Jesus. In this way the Eucharistic celebration is not only the fount but, in faith, it is also the apex of the whole Christian life (Church, 11:2), for it is a guaranteed situation of community growth.

4. The Eucharist and Community Growth

The Eucharist is the center of all group asceticism because it manifests, to the glory of God, a unity already achieved by the concrete efforts of the celebrating group. At the same time, each member of the group pledges himself or herself to future increased efforts in community growth toward unity. If within the community someone is not prepared to dedicate himself or herself to a future of intensified service for those who share the meal, then it would be inauthentic to celebrate a sacrament which is essentially prophetic of mutual commitment. How sad that frequent disagreement regarding the form of the Eucharistic celebration sometimes leads to an inability to live its essence. Some groups, because of their frame of mind and attitude of non-involvement in worship, actually make of the Eucharistic celebration a prophecy of a continued, widening gulf that divides participants.

If, on the other hand, we approach this community celebration in the way Jesus did, it would dynamically, socially, and sacramentally contribute to the spiritual growth of the group. Jesus says, "Now that you know this, happiness will be yours if you behave accordingly" (John 13:17).

In our reflections on the prayer of request, we pause to consider this unique communal act of thanksgiving, commitment, and service. Our Eucharistic prayer enables us to live out its promise, and urges us to request prayerfully that we realize this unity in our lives as believers.

CHAPTER FOURTEEN
Prayer as a Life of Communion with Jesus and the Father

Underlying many of the New Testament writings is the conviction that Christians experience a union with God in Christ. This relationship becomes the essence of our prayer and gives us confidence that our requests will be granted. In fact, we pray in the Lord and draw on this union as a source of our energy and a sign of our transformation in Christ. John's Gospel, known for its reflective approach, leads us to a deeper understanding of this communion and of its importance in our prayer.

1. Jesus' Gift of Life

John understands Christianity primarily as a new way of existence in a new age of God. It is above all a qualitatively new and different life. The Fourth Evangelist uses the term life more than the other three Gospels combined. He presents Jesus as the source of life: ''For as the Father has life in himself, so he has granted the Son to have life in himself'' (John 5:26). Jesus is like a Good Shepherd (John 10:14-15) who offers a loving revelation that brings salvation and life (John 1:17-18). John identifies Christ, salvation, and life. Thus, Jesus can claim, "I am the resurrection and the life. He who believes in me will live" (John 11:25), and "the one who feeds on me will live because of me" (John 6:57). Jesus is "the way and the truth and the life" (John 14:6) who, by laying down his life for those he loves, can claim, "whoever lives and believes in me will never die" (John 11:26).

John's new proclamation fulfills several purposes, among which is the fostering of faith. Prior to the addition of an appendix, John's Gospel ended by stating that the Gospel's aim was to aid people in believing that Jesus is the Messiah (John 20:31). This faith leads to a new life, as the last line of the original conclusion states so clearly, "by believing you may have life in his name" (John 20:31). Those disciples who believe pass from death to life (John 5:24). Jesus, the Good Shepherd, tells them, "I have come that they may have life, and have it to the full" (John 10:10).

Jesus brings new life and freely offers it to the disciple. No one earns it, but rather—with openness to God, belief, and acceptance of Jesus' words—the Lord gives new birth to this life from above. Once born again to this life with Jesus, the disciple lives in communion with Jesus: "Remain in me, and I will remain in you" (John 15:4). This mutual abiding is a new ongoing relationship, necessary for continued life and effectiveness: "I am the vine; you are the branches. If [anyone] remains in me and I in [that one], he [or she] will bear much fruit; apart from me you can do nothing" (John 15:5). This loving, faithful obedience to live in communion with Jesus produces the extraordinary pledge of Jesus: "If anyone loves me, he [or she] will obey my teaching. My Father will love him [or her], and we will come . . . and make our home with him [or her]" (John 14:23).

Jesus' gift of life leads to an experience of God. The disciple maintains this relationship with ongoing daily recommitment. John gives no ethical demands, nor does he present any ministry discourse. Rather, the disciple must believe, live, love, and pray as if these were four facets of the same new life of communion.

2. John's Theology of Communion

Jesus tells Nicodemus, ''God so loved the world that he gave his one and only Son, that whoever believes in him shall not perish but have eternal life'' (John 3:16). This abundant life (John 10:10), given because of love, is the great sign of Jesus' friendship (John 15:13). It is a life of faith in Jesus that leads to eternal life with him.

The Fourth Evangelist presents his theology of communion in the parable of the vine, in which the vinegrower is the Father, the vine is Jesus, and the branches are the disciples. Jesus is the true vine, and there is no suggestion of grafting on to the old vine of Judaism. Rather, a new life filters through to the branches. The Father cuts away unfruitful believers so that they do no damage to the growing vine, and he prunes the fruitful believers so that they might bear even more fruit. The power of Jesus' Word also cleanses those disciples who embrace this new life. They live with the awareness that they must daily and permanently draw sustenance from the vine, otherwise they will quickly become useless, wither, and die.

Besides an abiding union with the Lord, disciples must be faithful to the words of Jesus. Such union and fidelity lead to fruitfulness that gives glory to the Father. It is love that guarantees both the union and obedience that prove the quality of discipleship. Thus, the union between Jesus, and disciples is authenticated by the disciples' union among themselves. They become friends who deepen their love for each other as proof of their love for the Lord. Jesus calls these disciples his friends, tells them of the love of the Father, and assures them that he reveals to them all that the Father entrusts to him. The parable and discourse ends with the challenge to bear fruit, the promise of the Father's continued responsiveness to their prayers, and the call that ''This is my command: Love each other'' (John 15:17).

John's theology of communion is more than togetherness; it is a permanent mutuality of life and action between the Father, Jesus, and disciples. After urging disciples to feed on his flesh, Jesus succinctly states the basic dimension of the communion disciples share: ''Just as the living Father sent me and

I live because of the Father, so the one who feeds on me will live because of me'' (John 6:57). The relationship between Jesus and the Father is the model for the new life between Jesus and the disciples. On the feast of the Dedication, Jesus tells a group of unbelieving Jews that his miracles show that ''the Father is in me, and I in the Father'' (John 10:38), an idea he will later repeat to Philip (John 14:10-11). This communion of life and love extends to disciples through the indwelling of the Spirit: ''The Spirit of truth . . . lives with you and will be in you . . . Because I live, you also will live. . . . [Anyone] who loves me will be loved by my Father, and I too will love him [or her] and show myself to him [or her]'' (John 14:17-21).

This communion between disciples and the indwelling Father, Son, and Spirit produces an experience of profound knowledge permeated with love: ''I know my sheep and my sheep know me—just as the Father knows me and I know the Father'' (John 10:14-15). This illuminating experience is an anticipation of eternal life: ''Now this is eternal life: that they may know you, the only true God, and Jesus Christ, whom you have sent'' (John 17:3).

3. A Life of Communion Authenticated in Love

The new life that Jesus brings to his disciples is a life of communion with himself and with the Father, rooted in Jesus' own union with the Father. Love is the manifestation and authentication of this life of communion. In his final prayer during the Last Supper, Jesus expresses this profound link between love and the life he has revealed to his chosen ones: ''I have made you known to them, and will continue to make you known in order that the love you have for me may be in them and that I myself may be in them'' (John 17:26). Love permeates the plan of salvation, from the Father's creative love for the world (John 3:16-17) to Jesus' love for his own. Those people who distance themselves from Jesus have no love of God in their hearts (John 5:42), and Jesus does not even pray for them (John 17:9). However, to believers he says, ''As the Father has loved me, so have I loved you. Now remain in my love'' (John 15:9).

The Fourth Gospel is the only one in which Jesus speaks of the disciples' love for himself, a love inspired by the Father (John 8:42) and shown in obedience to Jesus' revelation (John 14:21). This faithful love produces a life of communion: ''Whoever has my commands and obeys them . . . is the one who loves me. [The one] who loves me will be loved by my Father, and I too will love him [or her] and show myself to him [or her]'' (John 14:21).

A manifestation of disciples' love for the Lord is prayer: ''If you remain in me and my words remain in you, ask whatever you wish, and it will be given you'' (John 15:7). The context for any prayer of request and an assurance of its answer in John is union with the Lord. Jesus is the Johannine community's model of prayer: praying in thanksgiving at Lazarus' tomb (John 11:41-42), for glory at the end of his ministry (John 12:27-28), in intercession for his disciples and future Church during the Last Supper (John 17:1-26). He always prays as Son in union with his Father. Jesus teaches his disciples to pray in Spirit and truth (John 4:23-24), to pray in his name (John 14:13-14), to pray for perseverance and fruitfulness (John 15:16), and to pray that ''your joy will be complete'' (John 16:24). The Johannine commandment to love Christ challenges disciples to make their faith concrete in loving obedience to Jesus and his words, and in prayerful dependence on his support.

The love to which a life of communion leads overflows to the community (John 13:34-35; 15:12-13). Jesus calls this a new command and challenges disciples, ''Love one another. As I have loved you, so you must love one another'' (John 13:34). Disciples must love each other with the quality of love that Jesus shows to disciples. In fact, Jesus sees this new command as a summary of all his wishes (John 15:12).

A disciple's love, rooted in Christ, is visibly demonstrated through service to others. This witnessing to love has extensive consequences: ''By this all . . . will know that you are my disciples, if you love one another'' (John 13:35). Jesus not only calls his disciples to love but also to a love that leads to a deep unity among themselves in community (John 17:11). He goes on to request in prayer, ''May they also be in us so that the world may believe that you have sent me" (John 17:21). The revelation of God's love leads to faith, faith that manifests itself in a love rooted in the unity of Father and Son. Love in the Christian community builds unity, and this unity leads others to believe in the revelation. Thus, this new command of love is the visible sign of disciples' faith, and both love and union become the focus of our requests made to God.

4. Ministry Results from this Life of Communion

Disciples share a sense of mission and ministry because of their union with Jesus. He could say, "My food . . . is to do the will of him who sent me and to finish his work" (John 4:34). Later, in prayer to the Father, Jesus says, "I gave them the words you gave me and they accepted them" (John 17:8). Provided the word of the Father remains in the disciples, they prolong the mission of Jesus. Thus, awareness of union is the basis of mission and ministry, a union maintained "If you remain in me and my words remain in you" (John 15:7).

Disciples sent by Jesus to proclaim his word serve him, follow him, and live united to him (John 12:26; 17:24). This implies sacrifice, imitating Jesus' humble service (John 13:1-11), embracing persecution (John 15:18-27) or even death (John 16:2), and following the Lord faithfully in whatever vocation God wills (John 21:18-23). Jesus' mission from the Father is "to testify to the truth" (John 18:37). During the Last Supper, Jesus shares this call with his chosen ones, telling them, "And you also must testify, for you have been with me from the beginning" (John 15:27). The disciples Jesus personally chooses (John 15:16) bear fruit, convinced that their witnessing will be fruitful if they maintain their deep union with him in loving obedience: "If anyone loves me, he [or she] will obey my teaching" (John 14:23).

The Fourth Gospel gives no missionary discourse, no handbook on discipleship. Rather, the evangelist's theology of communion is the basis for life, love, community, and ministry. Jesus himself is the model for this contemplative life of union from which all else flows. He lives in permanent union with his own Father. Jesus states that the Father taught him

(John 8:28), knows him (John 10:15), glorifies him (John 8:54), consecrates him (John 10:36), and sends him into the world (John 1:14). Jesus insists that his teaching is not his own but the Father's (John 7:16), and he asserts that God's works are manifest through him (John 9:3). Jesus lives in complete conformity with the Father's will (John 5:6), praying to the Father (John 12:27), expressing thanks for his gifts (John 6:11), and showing confidence that the Father will hear his prayers.

Jesus, who is always obedient to his Father (John 4:34), acknowledges that the Father gives success to his ministry (John 6:37, 44, 65). Jesus' unique experience of the Father (John 8:38) leads to mutual love and to his ministry (John 3:35). The mutual knowledge and love between Jesus and the Father is so profound that Jesus claims, ''I and the Father are one'' (John 10:30). Jesus reveals the Father to disciples (John 1:18), and the implications for discipleship are evident. Disciples must develop a profound communion with Jesus and thereby have access both to him and to the Father. Then, abiding in their love, the rest of life will take care of itself.

Communion, in this sense, is the basis of our Christian life. Any form of prayer rests on this realization and develops out of this unique presence.

CHAPTER FIFTEEN
The Spirit Who Prays Within Us

Our last reflection leads us to realize the quality of God's life within us. In the letter to the Romans, Paul reminds the community that "You . . . are controlled . . . by the Spirit, if the Spirit of God lives in you. And if anyone does not have the Spirit of Christ, [that one] does not belong to Christ. But if Christ is in you . . . your spirit is alive because of righteousness. And if the Spirit of [the one] who raised Jesus from the dead is living in you, [the one] who raised Christ from the dead will also give life to your mortal bodies through [the] Spirit, who lives in you" (Rom 8:9-11). More concisely, Paul states the same reality in 1 Corinthians: "[The one] who unites himself [or herself] with the Lord is one with [the Lord] in spirit" (1 Cor 6:17). In chapter twelve of the same letter, the Apostle uses such phrases as "the same Spirit," "the same Lord," "one and the same Spirit;" "All the members, though many, are one," since "all were made to drink of the same Spirit" (1 Cor 12:6, 13).

This rich terminology reflects Paul's understanding of Church and Christian life. We are not only united to Christ and to each other as members of his body, but as believers we are "in Christ," sharing his life and his Spirit. The Spirit given to all Christians is the same Spirit that is in Christ. Since all share this one Spirit, we become one person in Christ, and so the model of Church as the mystical person emerges. The many become the one Christ, because all share the same inner life principle, the Spirit.

Paul's use of the phrase "in Christ" expresses this intimate union of Christ and believers, but it also conveys the dynamic influence of Christ in our lives. Those "in Christ" can draw on the abiding presence and power of the Lord at all times. This insight directs our lives and our prayer. Believers live differently because of this identifying presence and union.

This union occurs because the "Spirit dwells in you" (Rom 8:11). Christians receive "the Spirit which is from God, that we might understand the gifts bestowed on us by God" (1 Cor 1:12). If we understand God's gift and "if we live by the Spirit, let us also walk by the Spirit" (Gal 3:25), for the Spirit transforms our existence: "And we, who with unveiled faces all reflect the Lord's glory, are being transformed into his likeness with ever-increasing glory, which comes from the Lord, who is the Spirit" (2 Cor 3:18).

This solidarity in the one Spirit challenges us to draw on the abiding presence of the Lord within us. The Spirit constitutes our existence as the one mystical person, the total Christ. Our realization of this union is an impetus to live out as community this new life in the spirit of Christ. The fact that we as Christians discover unity because of the indwelling Spirit, enables us to discern the Spirit's gifts for the transformation of our Christian lives on a day to day basis. This Spirit also prays within us, enabling us to articulate our deepest hopes and live out the implications of union in the Lord. Furthermore, this union in the one Spirit is not simply an individual reality, the Spirit in me, but an ecclesial reality, the Spirit in us as Church.

1. The Spirit Within Us

Paul reiterates to various communities his conviction of the gift of the Spirit. In numerous places he states that "hope does not disappoint us, because God has poured out his love into our hearts by the Holy Spirit, whom [God] has given us" (Rom 5:5); "But by faith we eagerly await through the Spirit the righteousness for which we hope" (Gal 5:5; 3:5); "I keep asking that the God of our Lord Jesus Christ, the glorious Father, may give you the Spirit of wisdom and revelation, so that you may know [God] better" (Eph 1:17); "For I know that through your prayers and the help given by the Spirit of Jesus Christ, what has happened to me will turn out for my deliverance" (Phil 1:19); "You became imitators of us and of the Lord; in spite of severe suffering, you welcomed the message with the joy given by the Holy Spirit" (1 Thess 1:6); "Therefore, [anyone] who rejects this instruction does not reject [a person] but God, who gives you [the] Holy Spirit" (1 Thess 4:8).

This well-founded conviction develops in other ways. The Apostle sees Christ himself as a life-giving spirit. We read in 1 Corinthians 15:45: "So it is written: 'The first . . . Adam became a living being; the last Adam, a life-giving spirit' " (*see* 2 Cor 3:6; John 6:63a). But this Spirit is an ongoing gift of God in the abiding or continuous presence of the Lord within us (Ezek 36:27, 14): "Don't you know that you yourselves are God's temple and that God's Spirit lives in you?" (1 Cor 3:16); "Do you not know that your body is a temple of the Holy Spirit, who is in you, whom you have received from God? You are not your own" (1 Cor 6:19). We are "filled with the Spirit" (Eph 5:18) who reveals God's message to us (1 Cor 12:3; Titus 4:1; John 14:26; 16:13). This Spirit is God's gift to us, a life-giving spirit dwelling within us; it is the Spirit of the risen Lord that we share because of our union with him.

This relationship has implications for prayer: "Because you are sons [and daughters], God sent the Spirit of [the] Son into our hearts, the Spirit who calls out, 'Abba, Father' " (Gal 4:6; *see* Rom 4:6). Not only are we able to formulate words about our relationship with God, but the Spirit helps us in our weakness, expressing our pleas according to the mind of God. In this sense, the Spirit within us enables us to identify authentic concerns in prayer since the Spirit prays within us. This realization leads to mutual respect for requests offered in a spirit of faith.

The Spirit's gift enables us to pray as integrated persons; that is, with the spirit and with the mind (1 Cor 14:15-16). This awareness of prayer creates holistic attitudes towards prayer and in prayer. Likewise, Christian prayer, inspired by the Spirit, is a formidable gift, akin to prophecy in the early Church (1 Thess 5:18-20; 1 Cor 11:4-5; 14:13-17; Rom 8:26-27; Eph 6:18). The Spirit groaning within us releases an energy in prayer that leads to new life (Rom 8:23). Indeed, Paul can say, "For I am convinced that neither death nor life, neither angels nor demons, neither the present nor the future, nor any powers, neither height nor depth, nor anything else in all creation, will be able to separate us from the love of God that is in Christ Jesus our Lord" (Rom 8:38-39). We also realize in prayer that all things do work together for good as we understand more fully the love of God (Rom 8:28).

When the Apostle speaks of the Spirit within us, he uses the image of temple: "Don't you know that you yourselves are God's temple and that God's Spirit lives in you? If anyone destroys God's temple, God will destroy [that one]; for God's temple is sacred, and you are that temple" (1 Cor 3:16-17); "Do you not know that your body is a temple of the Holy Spirit, who is in you, whom you have received from God? You are not your own" (1 Cor 6:19). The temple, a holy place, gives rise to the use of the spiritual body or person filled with the Spirit of the Lord (1 Cor 15:44). If this Spirit is our life, then the Spirit praying within prays in relation to our human interests. But these interests reflect not only our personal concerns, but those of the mystical person, the Church, of which we are a part. Such prayer within the community speaks to the deep conviction of the Church regarding its inner life.

Many difficult references in Scripture, interpreted in a communal sense, have as their basis the underlying notion of corporate person. This understanding of the "one in the many" underlies Paul's theology of the Spirit, ecclesiology, and views of Christian life. It opens new possibilities for our personal union with the Lord in prayer, but also sees this union as a reflection of our ecclesial identity. The atmosphere of prayer is the universal presence of the Spirit, and so we rightly pray "in the Spirit."

The Spirit within us is not only a presence but a power, an energy to transform us in our lives through prayer (1 Cor 2:4; 1 Thess 1:5; 2 Tim 1:7). As we become conscious of the gifts of God (1 Cor 2:12; John 4:10), our prayer opens us more fully to the Lord in our lives. Our requests heighten this awareness of the Spirit's presence.

2. The Spirit's Gifts: A Sign of Union

The Spirit within us is not only a life-giving Spirit, but also a giver of gifts: "We have different gifts, according to the grace given us. If [anyone's] gift is prophesying, let [that one] use it in proportion to . . . faith" (Rom 12:6). Paul, in fact, prays that special gifts be given to the community: "I keep asking that the God of our Lord Jesus Christ, the glorious Father, may give you the Spirit of wisdom and revelation, so that you may know [God] better" (Eph 1:17). In these passages, the Apostle indicates the relationship of gifts to faith and how the Spirit provides unique gifts of wisdom and revelation for our enlightened understanding of the Lord: "Therefore you do not lack any spiritual gift as you eagerly wait for our Lord Jesus Christ to be revealed" (1 Cor 1:7). Here, Paul states with confidence that all we need in life is ours through the Spirit.

However, we find the central passages on the Spirit's gifts in 1 Corinthians 12–14. In these passages, Paul affirms the variety of gifts (1 Cor 12:4-6), identifies specific gifts (1 Cor 12:8-10), recognizes these gifts as coming from the one Spirit (1 Cor 12:11), and uses the analogy of the human body to describe the relationship of these gifts (1 Cor 12:12-30): "There are different kinds of gifts, but the same spirit" (1 Cor 12:4); "All these are the work of one and the same Spirit, [given] to each one, just as [the Spirit] determines" (1 Cor 12:11). But we notice an underlying reality as we reflect on these biblical passages. Whether the gift be preaching with wisdom or instruction, the gift of faith or healing, the gift of prophecy or recognition of spirits, the gift of tongues or interpretation, the quality of love determines our ability to recognize and to use these gifts: "But eagerly desire the greater gifts. And now I will show you the most excellent way. If I speak in the tongues . . . of angels, but have not love, I am only a resounding gong or a clanging cymbal" (1 Cor 12:31–13:1).

However, the quality of Christian love spoken about by Paul is of a special order: "And now these three remain: faith, hope, and love. But the greatest of these is love" (1 Cor 13:13). It is everlasting love grounded in our reception of God's gift to us in Christ (Rom 8:16-18, 38-39). Understanding this gift that binds together all other gifts comes only with our continual openness to the Lord in prayer. When Paul speaks of specific gifts such as prophecy, tongues, and interpretation, he specifies the necessity of prayer: "For this reason anyone who speaks in a tongue should pray that he [or she] may interpret what he [or she] says" (1 Cor 14:13).

Not only is prayer essential for the recognition of gifts and their appropriate uses, but it is also primary for establishing a context for ongoing discernment. Through the gifts of the Spirit discerned in prayer, we recognize the word of God given to us (1 Cor 14:36). Hearing the word of God requires the listening associated with prayer, an openness to receive, to recognize, and to use this revelation for the building up of the community.

Paul expresses a challenge to the community in his reflection on the Spirit's gifts. He says to "Be ambitious for the higher gifts" (1 Cor 12:31), suggesting that we need to yearn for and pray for these gifts. Intercessory prayer in this regard is for the qualities that will build up the community of faith. However, community building also implies personal growth in love and prayer. The two go hand in hand.

The presence of charisms in the community witnesses to the presence of the Spirit in the community. This sign becomes valuable to those outside the community of faith, leading to the confession that Jesus is Lord. The actualization of these gifts also reveals the quality of prayer in the community—a prayer of praise and thanksgiving, with its freedom and spontaneity. Although we become aware of the presence of the gifts of the Spirit through prayer, the presence of gifts also reveals the depth of prayer in the community. Specific gifts, such as the gift of tongues, speaking of mysteries in the Spirit, is a form of praise rising upward to God. Interpretation of tongues allows the community to penetrate these mysteries, leading to other forms of prayer and its fruits in ministry.

Scripture continually affirms that the Spirit dwells in the community, and that we can discern the authentic presence of the Spirit of Christ. In his first letter, Paul exhorts the community in this regard: "Do not put out the Spirit's fire; do not treat prophecies with contempt. Test everything. Hold on to the good. Avoid every kind of evil" (1 Thess 5:19-22). His recurring admonition to test everything is an acknowledgment of the community's ability to discern the direction of its Christian life. This discernment requires prayer, sensitivity to the Spirit's movements, and insight into the mysteries of God. Christians are "taught by the Spirit, interpreting spiritual truths to those who possess the Spirit" (1 Cor 2:13). Because Christians have "the mind of Christ," they can judge all things (1 Cor 2:15-16), and test their response and direction (1 Cor 10:15), for the "Spirit searches everything, even the depths of God" (1 Cor 2:10). This discernment speaks to maturity within the community of faith, and Paul prays for this growth: "And this is my prayer: that your love may abound more and more in knowledge and depth of insight" (Phil 1:9). Union in the Spirit is powerfully manifested in these gifts within the community of faith.

3. Christian Life: The Fruit of Union

Union in the Spirit results in the transformation of our lives, for "the Spirit gives life" (2 Cor 3:6), and "where the Spirit of the Lord is, there is freedom" (2 Cor 3:17). Paul continually challenges the community along these lines: "Since we live by the Spirit, let us keep in step with the Spirit" (Gal 5:25). Walking in the Spirit results in identifiable characteristics: "the fruit of the Spirit is love, joy, peace, patience, kindness, goodness, faithfulness, gentleness, and self-control. Against such things there is no law" (Gal 5:22-23). Other fruits of the Spirit include a "ministry of the Spirit" that the Apostle describes as glorious (2 Cor 3:8). Union with the Spirit of the Lord results in a life transformed by this vivifying principle and extended through the service of others: "Whatever happens, conduct yourselves in a manner worthy of the gospel of Christ. Then, whether I come and see you or only hear about you in my absence, I will know that you stand firm in one spirit, contending as one . . . for the faith of the gospel'' (Phil 1:27); "Because of the service by which you have proved yourselves, [all] will praise God for the obedience that accompanies your confession of the gospel of Christ, and for your generosity in sharing with them and with everyone else'' (2 Cor 9:13).

The Spirit's presence in Christian life exists from the very beginning (2 Thess 2:13). Therefore, Christian life is an expression of this presence and power; it becomes a new life in Christ. Prayer itself, a prayer of union, opens believers to the richness and possibilities of Christian life. While the fullness is still to come, we actualize in part many dimensions of being in the Lord. Indeed the presence of the Lord leads to ministry, with effective ministry conditioned more by the power of the Spirit than by human achievement. Because of a contemplative penetration of the mysteries of the Lord, the believer and the believing community can live radically different lives in their world.

Prayer becomes the continual source of deepening union, of Christian witness, and of effective ministry. For New Testament writers, the Church is most itself when it is at prayer. But the prayer of union, the real gift of the Spirit within, expresses itself not only in special moments of contemplation, but in every moment of life. Because we share the one Spirit, which is the abiding presence of the Lord, we are constant witnesses to the potential of humankind.

The most revealing model of Church in the earliest New Testament writings is that of the corporate mystical person. This model reflects the reality that we share the one Spirit, and because of this union, we form one person in Christ. This spiritual reality, apprehended in prayer, results in gifts and fruits of the Spirit that witness to the transformation of life. The Church is most itself when it abides in the Spirit, and when it allows this reality to permeate its every statement, structure, and sign. Our union with the Spirit who prays within us, challenges each of us to reflect on the fruits of that union, seen in mutual respect, love, trust, and service, according to the gifts and insights of the Spirit. Emphasis on the life-giving Spirit we all share moves us to real unity and equality, rather than an emphasis on the distinctions we experience as members of the body of Christ.

As we rely on the Spirit praying within us, our prayers become expressions of our life—its reality and its potential. In this light we continue to make our requests known to God, knowing the solid foundation we have in Scripture.

Readings:

Crosby, Michael. *Thy Will Be Done*. Maryknoll, N.Y.: Orbis Books, 1977.

Doohan, Helen. *Leadership in Paul*. Wilmington, Del.: Michael Glazier, 1984.

Matera, Frank. *Passion Narratives and Gospel Theologies*. New York: Paulist Press, 1986.

Stanley, David. *Jesus in Gethsemane*. New York: Paulist Press, 1979.